SAINT PHILOMENA
THE
WONDER-WORKER

Saint Philomena, pray for us!

SAINT PHILOMENA

THE

WONDER-WORKER

by

Father Paul O'Sullivan, O.P.
(E. D. M.)

"The souls of the just are in the hand of God, and the torment of death shall not touch them . . . And though in the sight of men they suffered torments, their hope is full of immortality. Afflicted in few things, in many they shall be well rewarded: because God hath tried them, and found them worthy of himself."

—Wisdom 3:1, 4–5

TAN Books
An Imprint of Saint Benedict Press, LLC
Charlotte, North Carolina

Imprimatur: Canon Emmanuel Anaquim, V. G.
Vicar General
Lisbon, February 7, 1925

First published in February, 1927. Published in 1954 by The Catholic Printing Press, Lisbon.

ISBN: 978-0-89555-501-4

Library of Congress Catalog Card No.: 93-61563

Printed and bound in the United States of America.

TAN Books
An Imprint of Saint Benedict Press, LLC
Charlotte, North Carolina
2012

Come, spouse of Christ,
receive the crown which the Lord
hath prepared for thee for ever:
for the love of Whom thou didst shed thy blood.
Thou hast loved justice and hated iniquity:
therefore God, thy God,
hath anointed thee with the oil of gladness
above thy fellows. With thy comeliness
and thy beauty, set out, proceed prosperously,
and reign."

— Tract from the Feast of a Virgin Martyr,
The Roman Missal

CONTENTS

PUBLISHER'S NOTE

Sometimes a question arises about devotion to St. Philomena being no longer acceptable in the Church. This question comes up because on February 14, 1961, just prior to Vatican Council II, the Sacred Congregation of Rites in Rome issued an instruction that St. Philomena's feast day, August 11, was to be removed from all liturgical calendars (which would include the liturgical calendar of the universal Church as well as calendars of particular dioceses or congregations which might include special feast days). A number of other feast days were likewise dropped at that time.

This instruction was a liturgical directive. It was *not* a declaration that St. Philomena was not a saint, nor a prohibition of private devotion to St. Philomena.

Actually, at least in the United States, the instruction had little or no effect as far as the liturgy goes, for the Feast of St. Philomena had not been listed in the Missal for some years even prior to the instruction.

In any case, private devotion to St. Philomena is still very praiseworthy. It is our hope that a renewal of devotion to St. Philomena will lead to a great shower of graces and favors from Heaven—to lead, in turn, to the restoration of the Feast of St. Philomena throughout the universal Church.

—TAN Books
October 26, 1993

LETTERS OF
CARDINALS AND BISHOPS

Paço Patriarcal, Goa

My dear Reverend Father,

It was with most lively satisfaction that I read the beautiful life of St. Philomena published by you. I am one of the least but most sincere clients of this great Saint, having received through her powerful intercession most special favours, among them £8,000 for the Missionary Colleges.

I dedicated to her honour *our principal chapel.* I have also placed under her protection and that of St. Francis Xavier the pious Association of the Missions which I have established.

Aware of how potent is the intercession of St. Philomena with the Almighty, and also moved by sentiments of gratitude towards her, I heartily congratulate you on the publication of the life of the dear little Saint, venerated by the Roman Pontiffs themselves and so tenderly loved by that great Saint, the Curé of Ars.

I fervently hope that this book may have the widest possible circulation.

I remain, my dear Father,

Yours devotedly in Jesus Christ,
✠ *Theotonio*, Archbishop of Goa
and Patriarch of the Indies

Archbishop's House
Port-of-Spain, Trinidad
May 15th, 1926

My dear Father O'Sullivan,

I thank you very sincerely for the copy you sent me of *St. Philomena The Wonder-Worker,* which I read and admired very much. It is very attractive, well printed, the style is simple and the reading matter informative and deliciously compelling.

No one can read the book without becoming a client of the Saint. I lent it to a person who had a friend seriously ill with rheumatic fever, and thanks to the intercession of St. Philomena and Our Lady of Lourdes, the sick person was marvelously cured. I shall always recommend the book to our people here.

I remain, dear Father O'Sullivan,

Yours devotedly in Our Divine Lord,
✠ *John Pius,* Archbishop of Port-of-Spain

June 2nd, 1926
Archbishop's House

My dear Father Paul,

Thanks very much for the copy of *St. Philomena The Wonder-Worker* you so kindly sent me. I read it with keen interest. It is simply fascinating, well written and beautifully brought out. Anyone reading it is sure to develop a strong devotion to the Saint who has such a powerful influence with our Divine Lord.

I hope to spread the devotion to St. Philomena in

this Archdiocese. She has a large number of clients here already.

Wishing your Apostolate of the Press every blessing, I am, believe me, dear Father Paul,

Very sincerely yours,
✠ *Robert W. Spence,*
Archbishop of Adelaide

Archbishop's House
Westminster, London SW. 1
30th June, 1926

Dear Father O'Sullivan,

Thanks very much for the book on St. Philomena, which I trust will lead to an increase of devotion to the little Saint so closely associated with the Cure of Ars. Once more I beg God to bless the work of Catholic propaganda in which you are engaged. May God give complete success to all your efforts.

Your devoted servant in Christ,
✠ *Francis Cardinal Bourne*
Archbishop of Westminster

Patriarchal Palace
Lisbon, 18th of August, 1927

To the Rev. Father P. O'Sullivan.

Very Reverend and Dear Father:

We heartily approve and recommend the beautiful little book recently published by you entitled *St.*

Philomena The Wonder-Worker.

The book is full of interesting information, its teaching eminently practical, and its arguments carry with them conviction—based, as they are, not only on the authority of distinguished writers and scientists, but still more on the clear, categorical and repeated decisions of the Roman Congregations and the Declarations of the Sovereign Pontiffs themselves.

We, therefore, desire that the book have a wide circulation for the greater glory of God and for the honour of His servant Philomena. We grant 100 days indulgence to the faithful of this Patriarchate who read the book for at least a quarter of an hour each day.

I remain, my dear Father,

Yours devotedly in Jesus Christ,
✠ *António*, Cardinal Patriarch

Bishop's House
Middlesborough
18 January, 1929

My dear Father O'Sullivan,

Let me thank you very warmly for your goodness in sending me a copy of your excellent booklet entitled *St. Philomena The Wonder-Worker.*

Let me say at once that I am very pleased with your book, which is so calculated to spread devotion to the Dear Little Saint. There is a devotion to her in this diocese which I should like very much to increase. I should be so glad if you would order for me 100 copies of your book. We have a statue of the Saint in the Cathedral here. At St. Patrick's Church, Middlesborough, the Saint has her chapel, with a nice altar and statue, where she has worked many wonders. I feel sure your book will do much good in spreading the devotion to the Saint.

Yours sincerely in Jesus Christ,
✝ *Richard*, Bishop of Middlesborough

Foreword

A PRIEST AND A SOLDIER

The writer of the following short sketch [that is, this book] was himself at one time very little in sympathy with the "dear Little Saint," as the holy Curé of Ars loved to style St. Philomena. In fact, he strenuously opposed the erection of her statue in the church then under his direction. Happily, however, the Saint, in her own inimitable way, overcame with a sweet violence this unworthy opposition and transformed her would-be antagonist into one of her most grateful clients. This fact will go far to show how impartial is the testimony he bears to her.

The erection of her statue in his church was the signal for a shower of graces bestowed not only on him, but on the members of his flock, who speedily became convinced by personal experience that St. Philomena was, in truth, a most amazing wonder-worker and a most generous protector of all who have recourse to her.

Favors were multiplied, blessings followed in quick succession, graces of all kinds were granted in such abundance that verily the floodgates of Heaven seemed open. Frequently as many as fifteen lamps were seen burning before her statue, whereas the custom of the church had, up to then, allowed of but one lamp for each altar. When the same church was threatened with seemingly inevitable ruin, the Saint intervened and saved it from certain destruction in a truly wonderful way.

If the writer of the sketch is a priest, the kind friend who has undertaken to defray the cost of the publication is a soldier, who, no less than the priest, has reason to be grateful to the Little Thaumaturga.[1] Many and great are the favors he owes her—not the least of which: man's great ambition, "a happy marriage and a charming home." Very striking was the favor bestowed on him during the Great War. Though exempted for many reasons from going to the front, he nevertheless placed himself under the protection of the Saint, abandoned a flourishing business and joined the army as a simple soldier. Throwing himself into the work of the war with the strenuousness of an ardent patriot, he covered himself with glory and rapidly rose to the rank of Staff Major. In this capacity he enjoyed the highest esteem of his general and won the warm affection of his fellow officers. As a member of the artillery corps, he braved the greatest dangers. Yet amidst the most imminent perils he escaped unscathed, literally without a scratch. Finally, on leaving the army, instead of finding himself destitute, as was the fate of many thousands of his fellow officers, he speedily obtained a lucrative position very much superior to that which he had so generously abandoned. This new blessing he attributes to the never-failing kindness of his saintly Protectress.

In gratitude and love the priest and the soldier offer

---

1 Thaumaturge—miracle-worker. ("Thaumaturga" is a feminine form of the word.)—*Editor*, 1993.

to the public this little tribute of their devotion and affection.

—S.S.

OUR SOURCES OF INFORMATION

In compiling these short and unpretentious pages not a few works have been consulted, such as *Roma Soterranea* by de Rossi, which we consulted with reference to the Catacombs. The life of Pauline Marie Jaricot, whose marvelous cure at the Shrine of St. Philomena was one of the main reasons why the Saint's Office was granted to the Church, furnished us with the circumstances bearing on that subject. We perused with care the life of the Curé d'Ars because of his well-known devotion to the Saint and his wonderful recovery through her intercession. Finally, various works and pamphlets which bore directly on the Sanctuary or miracles of the Saint were put under contribution.

Personal experiences have been added, and facts gleaned during a prolonged visit to the Saint's Sanctuary at Mugnano are likewise embodied here.

Chapter 1

THE CATACOMBS

Who has not heard of the Catacombs of Rome—those wonderful, hidden passages and corridors, those subterranean chambers dug out in the bowels of the earth and forming, as it were, a belt of underground fortresses around and in the close vicinity of the Eternal City. After St. Peter's and a visit to the Holy Father, the Catacombs, with their hallowed memories, are the great sight of Rome. Here venerable Pontiffs, saintly Bishops, spotless Virgins, fearless Martyrs, gathered together in secret to celebrate the Divine Mysteries. Here too, tender youths and venerable old men, proud patricians and humble plebeians, nay princes even and slaves, knelt at the same altar, adored the same God, and participated in the same Divine Food.

Here they met in the evening at the feet of the venerable Pontiff; a few short hours after, they were fighting with lions in the arena, and when the darkness of the night again overshadowed the earth, their mangled remains were borne back for the last benediction to the feet of Christ's Vicar on earth. Then they were reverently enclosed in crypts hollowed out in the tufa granolare or soft stone, where, side by side, the living dwelt with the dead—these resting after

1

their labors, those awaiting their summons to the battlefield.

The meaning of the word "Catacomb" is not evident at first sight. It would seem to mean a depression or hollow in the ground, and we find it applied for the first time to a neighborhood in the Appian Way, close by the tomb of Cecilia Metellus, under which lay the cemetery of St. Sebastian. The name Catacomb, given to this cemetery, was then gradually applied to the others around Rome. The word thus came to mean a subterranean burial place dug out in the soft stone or tufa by the early Christians.

THE ORIGIN OF THE CATACOMBS HAS NOW BEEN THOROUGHLY INVESTIGATED

For many years it was commonly believed that they had been *sand-pits* from which, as the sand was extracted for building purposes, long passages and corridors were formed, which in the early ages of Christianity, the faithful used as places of refuge.

This opinion is no longer tenable. The great number of Catacombs are not dug out in the sandy soil, but hollowed out in the strata of soft stone common about Rome.

Moreover, sand-pits must of a necessity have been near the surface of the earth and they must have been so fashioned that the sand could be easily removed from them.

The Catacombs, on the other hand, are sunk deep in the earth—30, 40, or even 50 feet below the surface—and are reached by a steep stairway. They consist of long, narrow passages and corridors opening

out into crypts and chambers. These passages inter-
sect each other at different angles, and the corridors
so formed present a perfect labyrinth of ways and by-
ways, shooting off for long distances and again branch-
ing off into a new maze of streets and cross streets. At
intervals, shafts go down from the first set of chambers
deeper into the ground and open into new and lower
galleries, and others again, from these into still lower
depths, so that two, three, and even more tiers of passages and chambers lie, one under the other, forming
a very extensive underground city. It is not, therefore,
conceivable that these should have originally served as
sand-pits, as it would have been well-nigh impossible to
extract sand from them in the large quantities required
by Roman builders. The truth is that an entrance to
the Catacombs was sometimes made through one of
the sand-pits so as to avoid detection and to cover the
retreat of those who entered. It is also possible that
the sand-pits proper might have in the very first days
of persecution furnished hiding places for the perse-
cuted Christians, before they had time to prepare a
refuge for themselves, as they did shortly afterwards.

The Catacombs, therefore, as we know them, were
bored in the soft stone by the early Christians as places
of burial for their dead, and for the living as places of
refuge in time of persecution.

That they served admirably for these purposes is
evident. Firstly, the entrance was carefully concealed.
If this were discovered or its position made known by
some traitor, the approach of an enemy was speedily
discovered and frustrated by the faithful, who fled at
the first alarm into the more hidden recesses, where
pursuit was out of the question. For it needed not only

a perfect knowledge of the corridors, but the greatest circumspection to avoid being lost in the bewildering network of those dark passages, so closely resembling each other. Moreover, the corridors were so narrow that an excavator could in a few minutes throw up a barrier of sand and block them up effectually, thus rendering a chase absolutely impossible. As a final resource, some at least of the Catacombs were joined one with another by secret passages through which the fugitives could escape in an extreme necessity.

THE EXACT DATE OF THE FIRST CATACOMB IS NOT KNOWN

The pagans usually cremated their dead. This custom seems to have been abhorrent at all times to the Christians. Like the Jews, they preferred to bury their dead, according to the custom prevalent in Palestine, that is, in vaults cut out in the rock, such as we read of regarding the burial place of Lazarus. The Sepulchre which Joseph of Arimathea ceded for the burial of Our Lord was also hewn out of rock.

Since, however, the persecution started in the reign of Nero (A.D. 54-68), and the Christians could not safely perform the burial services in the presence of their heathen enemies above ground, it is clear that from a very early date indeed they must have begun to hollow out these subterranean cemeteries. We have proofs of the existence of the Catacombs certainly as early as the reign of Domitian, A.D. 96.

It is not easy to divine where the Christians who died in Rome before this date were buried. No traces of such burial places are to be found, but it is surmised that they were buried either in the Jewish cemetery, less abhorrent to them than pagan burial grounds, or that Roman converts who had private mausoleums allowed their new brethren to have a resting place in the immediate proximity of their own.

THE EXTENT OF THE CATACOMBS

The Catacombs are enormous in extent, and it is calculated that, if instead of being grouped around Rome they were stretched out in one direction, they should reach to a length of several hundred miles. Grave authorities tell us that six million Christians were buried in the Catacombs. The number is not excessive if we calculate that these cemeteries were in use upwards of 300 years and that in these 300 years 10 bloody persecutions were waged against the helpless Christians. Though the 60 Catacombs in the vicinity of Rome are the most famous, there are others scattered over different parts of Italy, France, Greece, Illyria, Africa and Asia Minor, all of which possess many notable archeological treasures.

WHY THE CATACOMBS WERE ABANDONED

The Catacombs were naturally abandoned when Constantine gave lasting peace to the Catholic Church. Hiding places were no longer required, and there was no further need for subterranean burial places. They were venerated however, and most justly so, as places of pilgrimage, for they were the hallowed resting places of the heroes and heroines whose names were in every mouth, whose memories were revered, whose combats and triumphs were the glory and consolation of the Church and whose help was invoked in every need.

Thus they continued until Rome fell prey to the Goths and Lombards. These barbarous invaders, believing that vast treasures were hidden in the underground vaults, invaded the sacred precincts, broke open the tombs of the martyrs and scattered their dust on the ground.

The next phase in the history of the Catacombs was marked by the transference of the relics of the more famous martyrs to the great Basilicas and other Sanctuaries especially erected for them by the Roman Patricians. The Popes, desirous of depositing these precious remains in places more worthy of them and anxious to put before the eyes of the people the examples of those heroes and heroines of the Faith, proceeded to transfer thousands[1] of the bodies to above-ground churches, where they would be more accessible to the veneration of the faithful.

The Catacombs, thus despoiled of their richest treasures, became gradually less and less frequented and at last were entirely abandoned. Dirt and debris so blocked the entrances that in a short time all knowledge of their whereabouts was lost to the world, and it was only in the year 1578 that they were casually re-discovered. The Roman Pontiffs now became thoroughly alive to the vast importance of safeguarding them and appointed trustworthy custodians to watch over the treasures still enclosed in them.

The present procedure is as follows: Expert

---

1 In the cemetery of St. Callixtus, 174,000 martyrs and 45 saintly bishops were buried. Pope Pascal I alone is said to have translated to the Church of St. Praxedes 2,000 bodies!

workmen, directed by learned ecclesiastics, are appointed to make excavations. When a new discovery is made, work ceases until the competent authority arrives, and then a minute examination commences under the direction of specialists. Everything on the exterior of the sarcophagus is first carefully noted, after which the sarcophagus is opened for the examination of what may be found inside.

Satisfied that they are in the presence of the relics of a holy Martyr, those present fall on their knees and recite the prescribed prayers. Then follows diligent investigation, and every sign or emblem discovered is described in writing for the better elucidation of the history of the martyr.

Chapter 2

THE FINDING OF THE BODY
OF ST. PHILOMENA

It was on May 24, 1802 that the excavators came on a loculus that had never been violated. Everything pointed to the fact that the chamber was exactly as it had been when the precious remains were enclosed there long centuries before. The discovery was looked upon from the first as something remarkable, and the opening of the sarcophagus was marked for the very next day, May 25.

On arriving at the spot, the learned custodian noted that the vault was walled up with three terra cotta slabs on which were depicted in red the symbols of martyrdom. They bore the following inscription:

LUMENA—PAX TE—CUM Fl

It would seem that the slabs had been misplaced, as happened so often in the necessary haste of burial. The first slab should have been placed in the third place and when this is done the inscription becomes at once clear:

PAX TE CUM Fl LUMENA
PEACE [BE] WITH YOU, PHILOMENA

This "loculus" [tomb] is considered an excellent specimen of its kind and is rendered exceedingly valuable by the inscription on it of the very name of the Martyr whose remains were therein enclosed, a fact of rare occurrence.

In addition to this inscription, there were various emblems painted on the slabs.

First, there was an anchor which, from its resemblance to the Cross, was looked on as an emblem of hope. It is also at times a sign of martyrdom, as anchors were fastened to the neck of some of the confessors when they were thrown into the sea. Some think that St. Philomena was cast into the river Tiber.

Second, there were two arrows, one pointing upwards and the other downwards. These, too, might betoken the kind of death which the martyrs suffered, as some were shot to death with arrows.

Third, there was a lance, which might have had a similar significance.

Fourth, there was a palm—the emblem of the martyr's triumph.

Fifth, and lastly, there was a lily, an emblem of purity.

Upon the opening of the tomb, the relics of a Virgin Martyr were found, with a glass vase containing a portion of her blood in a dried form.

The dried blood found in vials close to the martyrs' resting places have been subjected at various times to chemical tests and proved to be blood.[1] In the case of the blood of St. Philomena we have a far higher guarantee of its genuineness than any given by such process. The wonders wrought daily in and by this

---

1 Small vessels of aromatic spices, it is true, were also placed near the sepulchres with the intention of purifying the heavy atmosphere of the Catacombs. The two facts are independent of each other and are in no wise contradictory.

precious relic, and witnessed by countless pilgrims, as well as by keen ecclesiastical experts, furnish us with a supernatural proof of the authenticity of the relic.

The bones, the ashes and the blood of the Saint were carefully placed in a wooden case, which was closed and sealed in three places. This was borne above ground, where it was again opened and minutely examined by experts, among whom were doctors, surgeons and theologians.

The skull was found to have been fractured. The bones were apparently those of a girl, and the doctors surmised that she was twelve or thirteen years of age.

ST. PHILOMENA GOES TO NAPLES

Little indeed is known historically of our Saint previous to her glorious Martyrdom. Her real history commences when her blessed remains were found in May of 1802 after having rested in the obscurity of the Catacomb of St. Priscilla for upwards of 1,700 years.

After the final examination of the relics, a document was made out and placed in the case containing the remains. This was once more closed and sealed and deposited in the chapel or treasury where the bodies of saints and martyrs were kept, awaiting the Holy Father's orders for bestowal on some church. Three years later, namely, in 1805, the Bishop of Potenza arrived in Rome, accompanied by a humble priest from Mugnano del Cardinale, a village not far from Naples, in the diocese of Nola. During his stay in the Eternal City this good priest, Don Francisco di Lucia, did all in his power to achieve the great ambition of his life, namely, to secure the body of some Virgin Martyr for his church. To this end, he obtained permission to visit the Treasury of Relics, where at first he was perfectly unmoved. As he approached, however, the spot where the relics of St. Philomena were deposited, an indescribable emotion took possession of him, and he felt all at once a burning desire to obtain these precious remains.

Insurmountable difficulties arose. It was against the custom to bestow such treasures on a simple priest. His petition was absolutely and irrevocably refused. An intimate friend of his, seeing his distress, succeeded by personal influence in getting for him the body of another Saint, which he reluctantly accepted, in lieu of what he so earnestly craved for. During the negotiations for the relics, Don Francisco was consumed with fever, lost all appetite, and fell seriously ill. The Bishop of Potenza became seriously alarmed for his life.

One evening, while the good priest was brooding over his disappointment, a sudden inspiration came on him: He promised to take St. Philomena as his special patron and to take her to Mugnano, if only he could get possession of her relics. He was instantaneously cured. Both he and the Bishop were convinced that the cure was a miracle of the Saint. Shortly after, the apparently insuperable difficulties were removed and Don Francisco became the happy possessor of the ashes, the bones, and the blood of St. Philomena.

From this moment forward began an uninterrupted series of miracles and wonders, the like of which have been rarely or perhaps never seen in the history of the Church. The sick were healed, the dying restored to health, sinners were converted, and evil-minded men punished. Prodigies the most extraordinary, graces the most abundant, blessings the most copious were the daily fruits of the Little Saint's intercession.

The Bishop and Don Francisco, deeply grateful for the latter's wonderful cure, promised to take the holy relics in their own carriage and give them *the place of honor*. The day of departure arrived. The bustle and fuss of preparation drove the promise out of the heads of the travellers. One thing, however, they made perfectly sure of and that was that the relics were safe. They were placed under the seat occupied by the Bishop and securely fastened. Scarcely, however, had His Lordship taken his place in the carriage when he felt sharp blows on his legs. He was forced to get out, and gave orders to the coachman to fasten the box more securely. It was, however, perfectly clear to all present that the case was as secure as it could possibly be. Nothing could displace it. Very much surprised, His Lordship resumed his seat, but the blows became again so violent that he was once more forced to relinquish his place and leave the carriage. This gave occasion to new discussions and further examination. All now saw for themselves that the case was so well fastened that not even the violent jolting of the carriage could move it, yet the carriage had not moved a single pace. For the third time the Bishop took his seat—but in vain. Again he was smitten sharply on the legs and so severely hurt that he beat a hasty retreat, declaring that on no condition would he travel with the box where it was: "Rather," said he, "will I take it in my arms all the way" It was removed and given the place of honor in the front of the carriage, whereupon all trouble ceased, and the journey was begun. Only now did our travellers recollect their promise and at once recognized, in the unaccountable blows, the wish of the Saint that her rights should be respected. Full of reverence and awe, these holy men took off their hats and, with cheeks bedewed with tears, tenderly and repeatedly kissed the blessed relics.

The rest of the journey to Naples was happily made. Our travellers lodged in the house of a good friend, where the relics were encased in a statue of the Saint specially made for the purpose, and this in turn was placed in a casket of precious wood.

The lady of the house, who was suffering from an incurable disease of long standing, proceeded with the help of others to robe the statue in precious garments. While they were thus engaged, the face of the statue was seen to undergo repeated changes of expression, and the relics exhaled a most delightful perfume. Before leaving the family which had given her so warm a reception, St. Philomena restored to perfect health the good lady of the house, to the great joy of her friends, who had entertained the gravest fears for her life.

FROM NAPLES TO MUGNANO

After a short delay in Naples, our travellers resumed their journey towards Mugnano, where the news of their approach caused the liveliest emotion and the good people gathered in crowds to welcome their celestial Patron.

Various prodigies occurred during the short journey, which was made on foot and during the night. Finding the darkness too intense to proceed, the bearers of the casket called on the blessed Martyr for help.

Immediately a small break in the clouds allowed the light of the moon to fall on the road around the little procession, which was thus enabled to proceed with perfect safety.

Later on, as the procession was passing Cimitile, the relics became unaccountably heavy, causing the bearers great difficulty in carrying them. Cimitile in olden days had been the scene of countless martyrdoms and the Saint wished, it would seem, to tarry a little near the glorious battlefield bathed by the blood of her fellow martyrs.

The whole neighborhood was at this time suffering from drought, and the cry arose from the multitudes that came flocking from all parts to welcome the Saint: "If she really wishes to show her power, let her get us the rain we so much need." Almost immediately, torrents of rain poured down, to the delight of the peasant-folk, who saw in the fact a manifest answer to their prayer.

Still more striking was another prodigy. The group of travellers bearing the relics arrived in Mugnano as the dawn was breaking over the hills. The roads were now thronged with crowds gathered together from all the neighborhood. It was necessary to pause while the enormous throng was being mustered for the procession. At this moment, a mighty whirlwind arose and came sweeping over the hillside. So appalling was this tempest that the people were terror-stricken. The cry arose on all sides: "God and St. Philomena save us!" One of the priests, addressing the frightened people, bade them fear nothing, for the storm was stirred up by the demons, who recognized in Saint Philomena the same dauntless Virgin who had so confounded them

17 centuries before and who was now coming again to put them to shame and snatch from them their victims. Still the wind shrieked and whistled in the most alarming way, approaching rapidly the spot where the relics were resting. Here it suddenly stopped, as if held at bay by an invisible power, and instead of sweeping past, as one would naturally have supposed, it mounted into the air and disappeared. Again and again it recommenced with relentless fury during the procession, but was powerless to do the slightest harm to the people. All were amazed at its manifest impotence, for it failed to extinguish a single one of the lights that were borne by the side of the relics. For two whole days, this weird wind howled on the neighboring hills. Satan foresaw the graces that were to be so plentifully showered on this favored neighborhood and vented his rage in a vain display of baffled hate and fury.

A great change soon became visible in Mugnano. Blessings were granted in rich abundance; miracles of all kinds showed the wondrous power of the Saint; the faith of the people grew in intensity; and the Sanctuary soon became known far and wide by reason of the marvelous favors accorded to the pilgrims who flocked to the feet of the Little Saint.

Chapter 3

THE MARVELS OF MUGNANO

The night before the arrival of the relics at Mugnano, a poor man who had been compelled to remain in bed for several months, absolutely unable to work, hearing of the arrival of the remains of the Holy Martyr on the morrow, prayed fervently to the Saint during the night, begging that he might at least be able to see and kiss the precious relic. The Saint seemed deaf to his prayer, for the pains, far from lessening, became more intense. When, however, the bells announced the arrival of the sacred treasure, he dragged himself from bed in spite of his sufferings and made heroic efforts to go and meet the procession. On leaving the house, he was perfectly cured.

For nine days the crowds flocked unceasingly to the church to venerate the relics, the ninth day being marked by notable miracles.

A poor widow besought the Saint during Mass to cure her **crippled boy** who was unable to stand. At the elevation of the Sacred Host, the boy jumped up from where he was and ran to the urn of the Saint's relics to thank her for his cure. At the conclusion of the Holy Sacrifice, the child walked about the town, to the delight of the admiring throngs, who rang bells and beat drums and finally, seizing the boy, bore him in procession through the streets.

The report of this miracle brought still greater crowds to the afternoon devotions. A poor mother dipped her finger in the oil of the Saint's lamp and anointed the eyes of her **little child** who had lost his sight from smallpox and whom the doctors declared incurable. The moment the mother anointed the lids, the child recovered its sight.

A freethinker was so profoundly moved at the sight of this new prodigy that he had the blessed light of faith restored to him. He declared himself a believer and gave large donations for the building of a church in honor of the Saint.

Some days later, a lady brought her **crippled daughter** to the Sanctuary and, cutting off the child's curls, hung them near the urn of the Saint's relics, making at the same time a generous offering to the Sanctuary. There was no apparent response at the moment, but on her return home the child, to the amazement and delight of all present, left the carriage and walked into the house. She had regained the perfect use of her limbs.

A blind man came and gave a valuable ring as an ex voto offering, confident that he would be cured. Nothing happened in the Sanctuary, but on reaching home, he recovered the full use of his eyes.

A blind girl, twenty years of age, whom the Neapolitan doctors declared beyond the reach of all human aid, came to Mugnano. Entering the church, she declared that she would not leave it until she was cured.

Her faith was put to a rigorous test, for all her prayers seemed in vain. She, on her part, only grew more persistent and refused to leave the church for dinner. In the evening, when the Sanctuary was being closed, she found herself obliged to seek a lodging for the night. Lo! As she was leaving the church, a faint glimmer of sight was given her. Next day she returned and remained the whole day in prayer. Again, on leaving at night, she saw much better, but still imperfectly. On the third day, about noon, she saw more clearly still. At evening time her sight was entirely restored so that she threaded a small needle with the finest thread.

Cures of body and mind now began to follow in quick succession, not only in the Sanctuary but at great distances from it.

A young mother was suffering **intense pains when giving birth** to her child. Unfortunately, she was all alone. A beautiful young girl suddenly appeared by her side and asked if she could do anything to help her. Her presence itself proved enough to allay all pain. When the young girl took her leave, the poor woman asked her name. "I am Philomena; they call me Philomena of Mugnano." The appearance of the Saint was so natural that it did not awaken the smallest suspicion in the mind of the sufferer of who she really was. On telling a friend of the unexpected visit, she learned that a Saint of that name had come to Mugnano from Rome. When she was better, accompanied by her friend, she made a pilgrimage to the Sanctuary. Glancing at the image of the Saint, she at once exclaimed: "It is she! It is she! Yes, she was my celestial visitor!"

A distinguished lawyer of Naples, Don Allessandro Serio, who had a property near Mugnano, suffered for many years from **a dangerous internal illness**. He and his wife came to Mugnano to beg for his cure.

They followed all the exercises of the novena which was being celebrated. The Saint, however, seemed deaf to their supplications, for on the 8th day of the novena, Don Allessandro was taken ill, and he had to be removed to his lodgings, where he speedily sank into unconsciousness, so that he was unable to make his confession. His wife, in the extremity of her grief, seized a picture of St. Philomena and called on the Saint for help. She only asked that the invalid might be able to confess, for she now despaired of a cure, which in all truth seemed impossible. She promised a marble altar to the Saint if this favor were granted. Scarcely had the prayer been made, when Don Allessandro regained his senses and began his confession, during which he was completely restored to health.

Mindful of the promise, the altar was ordered to be made. A new wonder was in store for the happy couple. One of the masons, when giving the last touches to the table of the altar, struck it so roughly that, to the consternation of all, it was broken in two pieces, leaving between the parts a **large fissure** fully the width of a finger. The unfortunate workman tried to remedy the break with cement, but the Little Saint herself came to the rescue, and the marble became most perfectly joined, leaving only a line or vein as a mark of the prodigy. This wonder was testified to by many witnesses, and an inscription commemorating it was placed in the church.

Louis of Mariconeoit, a Frenchman, married an English girl. The marriage proved to be an ideally happy one. But the joy was short-lived, for after six months, the young bride became seriously ill. She earnestly longed for **the happiness of being a mother**, but the doctors declared that her state of health made such a thing absolutely impossible. The young couple came to the neighborhood of Naples in the hope of a cure. Unfortunately, any little hope they had entertained was soon rudely dispelled. The patient's condition grew rapidly worse. Hearing of the marvellous cures wrought at Mugnano, she shut herself up one day in her own room and, falling on her knees, poured forth this short and fervent prayer to St. Philomena: "Since my condition is desperate, from the human point of view, and since I have no earthly hope left, I place all my confidence in you and trust that you will cure me, for you are powerful in Heaven and are good to all who seek your help. Despite my sufferings, I will go tomorrow to visit you in Mugnano, and I will ask you not only to restore me to health but to grant me the blessing of becoming a mother, and I will give my child the name of Philomena. Moreover, I promise to direct all the yearnings of its young heart towards God."

The following day, she visited the Saint's shrine and made her prayer with great confidence. A year later, she returned in perfect health, the happy mother of a beautiful child. Countless mothers like her have to thank St. Philomena for similar favors.

His Lordship, the Bishop of Lucena, was much in need of a professor of sacred eloquence for his diocesan seminary. The priest on whom his choice fell was Canon Vincent Redago. But the appointment was manifestly impossible, for the Canon was far advanced with **consumption** and already had frequent **hemorrhages**. His state was so grave that he was preparing himself for death, which he recognized could not be far distant. What was the good man's surprise when the Bishop announced his nomination! "What, my Lord!" he exclaimed, "have you the power to cure me?" "No," replied the Bishop, "I have not, but there is someone else who has. See, I bring you a picture of Saint Philomena. Recommend yourself to her and you will get the health necessary to perform the duties I impose on you." The Canon took the picture and placed it lovingly on his breast. He was instantly cured and perfectly able to undertake the task placed on him by the Bishop.

A young sculptor **lost the use of speech and hearing** for close to 20 years. Aware of the prodigies wrought by the dear Thaumaturga [miracle-worker], he made a novena to her during Holy Week. It was in the year 1837. On Holy Thursday night, he seemed to see St. Philomena surrounded by a throng of heavenly spirits and smiling at him. Delirious with joy, he uttered a great cry—he was cured. Shortly afterwards he went to Mugnano to pour out his grateful thanks at the Shrine of his heavenly benefactress.

A good Irish lady was sorely tried by God. To her great grief, **four children, one after the other, were born dead.** When the fifth was expected, she was filled with consternation and begged her sister, a nun, to pray for her. Her sister replied by recommending a novena to Saint Philomena, in which she herself promised to join. Shortly afterwards, a beautiful child, full of life and health, was born. In accordance with her promise she called the child Philomena.

A happy home is the reflection of Heaven, and the love which unites the members of a Christian household is a foretaste of the never-ending bliss of the Father's home above. The Baron and Baroness of

Lepore were blessed by God with supreme happiness. The union and love which bound these two hearts together was indeed enviable. A great trial, however, was in store for the happy couple. The health of the Baroness began to fail, and soon **a fatal illness** manifested itself. Medical skill proved unavailing. Remedy after remedy failed to check the course of the disease, and soon death became a question of moments. The feast of the Translation of St. Philomena's relics was being celebrated for the first time in Terlizzi, near the castle where the Baroness lay dying. As life was slowly ebbing away, a friend hastened there with an image of the wonder-working Saint. The Baron eagerly seized it, showed it to the dying lady and touched her with it. She was cured so perfectly that both husband and wife were enabled to start a few days later for Mugnano to thank the dear Little Saint.

The devotion spread rapidly all over Italy passing from city to city, from town to town, penetrating even to remote villages. Children received her name in Baptism; the poorest peasants kept lamps burning before her picture: chapels were built, statues erected in her honor; and in whatever town, village or church she was honored, wonderful prodigies and cures were wrought, and the moral condition of the inhabitants speedily underwent a radical transformation. In one church alone, within a few months after the devotion began, 1,200 silver ex votos were offered at her altar, besides many others of gold, jewels and precious stones—an eloquent testimony to the graces bestowed. In another, the cures, conversions and prodigies were so numerous that it was commonly said that nothing more wonderful happened in Mugnano itself.

Chapter 4

THE GREAT MIRACLE
OF MUGNANO

One of the most illustrious heroines which the Church has given to the world in modern times is without doubt the sweet French girl, Pauline Marie Jaricot.

Many were the obstacles which this noble child had to confront while following the high but arduous career marked out for her by God. She was the favorite daughter of wealthy parents, from whom she inherited a vast fortune. Her beauty was striking and singled her out in the most fashionable gatherings as an object of admiration. Added to this, she was clever, bright and gay, gifted with a most attractive personality and possessing a heart overflowing with gentleness and affection.

Everything in the girl drew one towards her. Society was at her feet. Notwithstanding the allurements of pleasure and the soft flattery of many friends, Pauline always felt a call to higher things. God beckoned her one way, the world another. This first combat was long and fierce, but at last grace triumphed, and the victory was for God.

The next struggle that our heroine was destined to encounter was of a far different nature. She lost her beloved mother at an early age and, at the same time,

25

fell herself prey to a violent disorder which attacked both body and mind, leaving her a veritable caricature of her former self. This trial, like the former, was long and intensely painful.

After this came a breathing space, which in turn was followed by a still more grievous malady, which kept her for long years at the very gates of death.

Wonderful are the ways of God, who ever purifies in the crucible of suffering the souls which He has chosen for great designs. It was this sorely tried child who was to give the Church three of its most important modern associations, each of which is gathering into the fold of Peter millions of abandoned souls.

Her first work was the foundation of **the Living Rosary**, the fruits of which are incalculable. **The Society for the Propagation of the Faith** came next. This society infused, in an incredibly short time, new life and vigor into the foreign missions and extended still further their already vast radius. By a simple system—the inspiration of Pauline herself—abundant funds flowed in from all parts, enabling the missionaries to achieve results far in excess of their wildest dreams.

Finally, if not the sole Foundress, she at least took a leading part in the establishment of **The Holy Childhood**, an association which is annually rescuing countless babes from the horrors and degradation of paganism.

Pauline's life story is well worth perusal, not only because it is teeming with interest, but much more because it sets before us an example which might well serve as a model and stimulus to other girls who, like her, could do great things for the world had they only the necessary confidence in God and themselves.

Unfortunately, it does not come within the scope of this work to give a more lengthy account of Miss Jaricot. We refer to her merely because of her connection with St. Philomena, by whom, as we shall see, she was miraculously restored to health and whose devotion she was instrumental in spreading all over France, and indeed, throughout the world.

We entitle the cure of Miss Jaricot **"the great miracle of Mugnano,"** firstly, because the Holy Father Gregory XVI, who was a witness of it, declared it to be a miracle of the first class; secondly, because it was the immediate reason why the Office and Feast of the Saint were granted to the universal Church; and lastly, because, more than any other of the wonders worked at Mugnano, it served to make the name of St. Philomena known far and wide.

We shall allow the young heroine to recount in her own words the history of her illness and the miraculous nature of her cure.

PAULINE'S ILLNESS

"It would be well-nigh impossible to describe the sufferings I endured for the past ten years. I do not pretend to give a scientific explanation of all I went through. I merely state what I felt and what I heard the doctors say.

"Up to March, 1835, I was as a rule able to bear my pains in such a way that those around me had no idea of what I was going through. After the Revolution [of 1831], however, the disease showed unmistakable signs of aggravation. As my malady chiefly affected the heart, in proportion as it increased, the **palpitations** became more violent, so that they could be heard at a distance. On these occasions, my sides heaved with the agony I endured. A slight movement or change of position was sufficient to send the blood rushing violently back to my heart, thus causing imminent risk of suffocation. My breathing seemed to cease and the beatings of my pulse became imperceptible, so that the most drastic remedies had to be applied to restore some degree of heat to my frozen limbs. The abnormal dilation of my heart compressed the lungs, and breathing became a positive torture. As a consequence, I was compelled to lie perfectly still, lest the over-charged blood vessels should burst.

"In the part of my chest where the palpitations were most violent, a cavity was gradually formed, into which the food that I attempted to swallow lodged, causing still further danger of suffocation. The doctors now made two openings in my side, in a vain effort to check the progress of the disease and with a view to lessen the danger of suffocation. I was in consequence reduced to such a state of pain and exhaustion as made it evident that death could not be far off.

"During these **awful years of torture**, I had some short intervals of relief. The most appreciable of these was at the end of a novena made to St. Philomena. The body of this Virgin Martyr had been recently discovered in the Roman Catacombs, and the marvels wrought by means of her precious relics were so extraordinary that the name of Philomena was on every tongue. At the mention of this dear name, I experienced intense joy and longed to kneel at the shrine of this illustrious Virgin. But alas! Such a thing seemed impossible, for her sanctuary was far away in Naples and I was unable to bear the least fatigue. Yet I felt inspired to go to the Sanctuary of the Sacred Heart at **Paray-le-Monial**, not indeed to ask for a cure, but to settle the affairs of my soul. Utterly worn out with pain, I said to myself: 'I survived the fearful shock and excitement of the bombardment, and though weeks and months have passed, I am still alive. Surely there is some hidden design of God's Providence in all this.' I knew that the Association of the Living Rosary was praying for me; so, placing my trust in God and these good prayers, I resolved on a step which, had it been known, would certainly have been deemed pure and simple madness.

"In fact I had some scruples about the matter myself as I had no wish to do anything of which my conscience did not fully approve.

"I therefore elicited from the doctor the information that my state was so desperate that nothing I might do mattered much one way or another. This declaration set my scruples at rest.

"When I mooted the project I had at heart, I met at once with opposition. Though he was not aware of it, I heard the doctor say in a whisper: 'Let her alone, let her go, she will not go far.'"

THE DIFFICULT JOURNEY

The preparations for the projected journey had been made in secret, so Pauline started immediately in a carriage for **Paray-le-Monial**, accompanied by her chaplain, a young lady friend and a confidential servant. The few who knew of her departure said: "She will not reach the first resting place alive." Even those who accompanied her feared that every jolt of the carriage would cause her death. However, no such thing happened.

She arrived safely at her journey's end and settled the affairs she had so much at heart. Then she said to herself: "This first journey did not kill me, so let me go to **Rome** and get the Holy Father's blessing." This was the ambition of her life.

If we think of what a journey to Rome meant in those days of coach-traveling over the Alps, through wild and abandoned stretches of territory infested with brigands, we shall be able to form some idea of the heroic faith and magnificent courage of this young girl. The journey was at all times wearisome and full of danger, but for one in Pauline's state of exhaustion and with so small an escort, it was perilous in the extreme. Death seemed to dog the steps of the travellers. The pains endured by the poor invalid were excruciating. Only when her sufferings were most intense could she be induced to make a short halt, and even then, after the briefest rest, she would insist with indomitable courage on pursuing the journey. When the party reached Chambery, Pauline herself lost hope and resigned herself to die far from home and far from the Vicar of Christ. Her weakness was extreme, and she completely lost the use of her senses, remaining unconscious for two whole days. The pupils in the convent of the town made a novena to St. Philomena for her recovery, and at its conclusion, she was much better and the journey was resumed. The snow was so deep on the road over the Alps that, notwithstanding their powerful horses and the valuable aid of sturdy mountaineers, their progress was slow and difficult.

As they reached the summit of Mount Cenis, a

glorious view burst on their delighted gaze, and they halted for some time to contemplate the magnificent panorama that stretched before them.

As they gazed on this wondrous scene, **a beautiful child** suddenly appeared—no one knew whence he came—and approaching the carriage where Pauline lay, smiled on her sweetly and presented her with a beautiful white rose, which exhaled a delightful perfume. The guides had never before seen the child, who disappeared as quickly as he had come, nor could they form any idea of who he might be. The rose, they declared, could not have bloomed in the mountains. No such flowers were found in these regions of snow. The little incident was a consolation for the travellers after all they had undergone. Pauline's companions saw in it a symbol of the beautiful present she was about to make the Holy Father—nothing less than the gift of her first great work, the Living Rosary, of which the white and fragrant rose was so fit an emblem.

"On our arrival in the Italian plains," she goes on to write, "we were forced to travel by night, as the heat of the day was excessive. I had no fear of brigands or of evil spirits since we were under the protection of Our Lady and St. Philomena. We made sure to have their medals hung on the carriage, and we likewise gave one to the postilions. It was eleven o'clock at night when we reached the foot of the mountain of Loreto, and though warned that the roads were not safe, we pushed on in the hope of soon reaching the House of the Holy Family (now the Basilica of Loreto), which we did as the dawn was breaking over the hills."

Here again the invalid had **a serious relapse**, and once more all hope was lost of saving her life.

Nevertheless, she rallied and after a few days' rest started anew on the road to the Eternal City. During this last stage of her journey, the attacks were frequent, and she arrived in **Rome** in an almost unconscious state.

The nuns of the Sacred Heart at the Trinitá dei Monti received her with the greatest affection. Her weakness was extreme, and it was simply unthinkable that she should leave the convent. Thus, after a long and perilous journey, in which she had braved so many dangers and even death itself, she had to halt at the very threshold of the Vatican. She could go no further.

The Blessed Mother and St. Philomena were with her, and she was not to lose her reward. The Holy Father soon heard of her arrival in Rome and, aware of the state of exhaustion in which she lay, resolved with truly paternal affection to go himself and visit his "dear daughter" whom he so tenderly loved and who deserved so well of Holy Church.

INTERVIEW WITH THE HOLY FATHER

It was surely an extraordinary honor, but a still more extraordinary consolation, for this most humble girl to receive the visit of the Vicar of Christ, who came expressly, not merely to visit and console, but to thank and bless her.

The Holy Father opened his great heart and poured forth his thanks in the most affectionate terms. He told his "dear child" how pleased he was with all she had done; he praised her great courage and ardent faith in coming to Rome, and blessed her most abundantly. It was like a visit of Our Blessed Lord, for in His Vicar she saw and reverenced the Master Himself. Seeing how exhausted she was, he asked her to pray for him when she got to Heaven.

"Yes, Holy Father," she replied, "I promise to do so, but if on my return from Mugnano, I come back well and go on foot to the Vatican, will Your Holiness deign to proceed without delay with the final inquiry into the cause of St. Philomena?"

"Yes, yes, my daughter," replied the Pope, "for that indeed would be a miracle of the first class."

Turning to the Superioress, the Holy Father said in Italian: "How ill our daughter is! She seems to me as if she had come forth from the grave. **We shall never see her again.** She will never return." Pauline understood what he said but only smiled confidently.

When leaving, the Pope blessed her anew and said to Cardinal Lambruscini, who accompanied him: "I recommend my dear daughter to you. Grant her all the indulgences and privileges it is possible to bestow."

It was now August, and the heat was terrific. The little party started for Mugnano, but had to travel by night and rest by day. They arrived at the Sanctuary on the eve of Saint Philomena's feast.

MUGNANO AT LAST

The Neapolitans and the crowds from all the surrounding districts who flocked to the Sanctuary for the feast went wild with excitement when they heard who Pauline was and why and whence she had come. Their sympathy for her on the one hand, their jealousy for the reputation of their dear Patroness on the other, awakened the highest enthusiasm. Here was **this**

French lady, so loved by the Holy Father, who had done so much for religion, come hundreds and hundreds of miles, over the snowcapped Alps, through mountain fastnesses, braving perils and death itself to invoke St. Philomena. She must, she must be cured!

"Dear St. Philomena," they cried, "you must cure this dear lady who has come such a distance to ask your aid. She has done enough for God and for the Madonna for you to cure her." And then, knocking at the urn of the Saint, as it were in threatening tones, they called out, "Do you hear us, Philomena! If you do not grant our prayer at once, we will invoke you no more; it will be all over between us. So much the worse for you, great Saint!"

The uproar became so terrific that Pauline could scarcely endure it.

THE MIRACLE

The next day, the feast itself, when Pauline received Holy Communion near the urn of the Saint, she experienced such **frightful pains** all over her body, and her heart beat so violently that she fainted away. At the sight of what they thought was death, the crowds gave way to such cries and vociferations that it was thought safer to carry the chair on which Pauline was lying out of the church. However, she regained consciousness enough to make a sign to be left near the urn, on which she fixed her eyes with an expression of the deepest affection. Suddenly, an abundant flood of hot tears burst from her eyes; the color came back to her cheeks; a warm, healthy glow spread through her benumbed limbs. Her soul was inundated with such heavenly joy that she believed that she was about to enter Heaven. But it was not death, it was life; Philomena, the beloved, had cured her, and she was preserved for long years of toil and labor, which were to end in a glorious though bloodless martyrdom.

Although she felt that she was cured, Pauline dared not for some moments reveal the fact, dreading the outburst of enthusiasm that it was certain to provoke. However, the Superior of the Sanctuary, understanding what had happened, ordered all the bells to peal and announce the miracle.

The crowds, on hearing the news, went frantic with joy and were absolutely beside themselves with delight. The church and the streets rang with their shouts. Vivas, vivas resounded on all sides. It would be impossible to describe adequately this magnificent and soul-stirring demonstration of faith. **"Viva St. Philomena!** Viva our dear Saint! Viva the great Virgin and Martyr! Viva the good French Lady!" In their wild enthusiasm they rushed towards Pauline and wanted to carry her in triumph on their shoulders. This, however, she absolutely refused to allow.

Idolized by the people, Pauline tarried in Mugnano for some time, her soul overflowing with joy. She passed long hours in sweet colloquy at the feet of her heavenly benefactress, and great were the graces she received, more even for soul than body. At last, when the day of departure arrived and she had to tear herself away from the Sanctuary, she took with her **a great relic of St. Philomena**, which she placed in a life-sized statue of the Saint. This was clad in royal robes, given the seat of honor in the carriage and was hailed by all as the "Princess of Paradise."

At the various stages of the journey, the postilions who had brought Pauline to Mugnano—more like a corpse than a living person—cried out "A miracle, a miracle! Viva St. Philomena!" At this cry, crowds used to gather, bringing wreaths and garlands which they hung on the carriage, invoking at the same time the name of the Saint with the most intense piety and love.

Naples was profoundly moved on the arrival of the miraculée. A thrill ran through the people. The Bishop received Pauline with great honor and, in the presence of the Apostolic Nuncio and the King of Sicily, presented the blood of St. Januarius for her to kiss and venerate.

Blessed and invoked on all sides, the "Princess of Paradise" and her escort soon arrived in Rome, where, the better to enjoy the Holy Father's surprise, Pauline had not announced her cure.

ROME AGAIN

When in the full enjoyment of health and strength she presented herself in the Vatican, all those who had heard of her were thunderstruck. "Is it really my daughter?" said the Holy Father. "Has she come back from the grave, or has God manifested in her favor the power of the Virgin Martyr?" "It is indeed I, most Holy Father," she replied, "whom Your Holiness saw so recently at the very door of death and on whom St. Philomena has looked with pity. Since she has given me back my life, deign, Holy Father, to give me permission to build a chapel in honor of my benefactress."

"Most certainly," replied the Pope, in accents full of joy and affection.

Then he insisted on hearing from her own lips the details of the cure. In his delight and wonder, he ordered her to walk up and down in his presence. "Again, again, quicker, quicker!" he exclaimed, laughing. "I want to be sure that what I see is not an apparition from the other world but really and truly my dear daughter from Fourvière." And as his dear daughter walked backwards and forwards, she naturally, without meaning it, turned her back on the Pope. The Master of Ceremonies hastily reminded her that she must not turn her back on the Holy Father, whereupon the Pope said with a smile: "Nonsense! Do not trouble about that. God Himself has made far greater exceptions in her favor."

The Sovereign Pontiff now ordered Pauline to remain in Rome for a whole year, that the miracle might be thoroughly investigated, during which time he conferred on her many and great privileges and gave orders for an immediate inquiry to be made into the cause of St. Philomena.

At the close of the year, with the blessing of Christ's Vicar, Pauline returned to Fourvière in France.

Chapter 5

A VISIT TO MUGNANO

In 1909 I had the happiness of visiting the Sanctuary of St. Philomena, bearing a letter of introduction to the custodians from the Papal Nuncio in Portugal, Monsignor (afterwards Cardinal) Tonti.

The good nuns, to whose care the Sanctuary of St. Philomena is committed, received me with such marked kindness and were so anxious that I should know everything about their great Saint that I was induced to prolong my stay for nine full days, listening with pleasure to the many beautiful incidents which the good guardians were pleased to recount. I spent a great part of each day in the Church of the Saint, and the good religious gave me every facility for venerating the precious relics as often and for as long as I pleased. Sometimes I accompanied the pilgrims who had come from afar and, with them, examined and kissed the reliquary containing the blood of the Martyr. Sometimes, when the chaplain was not present, it was my privilege to offer the relic for the veneration of the visitors, and frequently, when the church was closed, I was allowed to extract it from its repository for my private devotion.

THE BLOOD OF THE SAINT

The blood is not in a liquid state but quite dry and in appearance resembles ashes. It is preserved in a small crystal vase which allows the visitor to see it as perfectly as though it lay on the palm of one's hand. I had the happiness of examining this priceless treasure as many as thirty or forty times. Each time, without fail, I saw the blood change most marvellously, and the transformation was so clear and distinct as not to allow room for the smallest doubt or misconception.

Precious stones, rubies and emeralds, pieces of gold and particles of silver appeared mingled with the blood. One might shake the reliquary, and again the precious stones appeared, not always in the same way, but still clearly and distinctly. At times, too, small black particles appear, which are supposed to presage some cross or affliction or foretell impending evils. These black particles were very noticeable when the great Pontiff, Pius IX, venerated the blood of the Saint and were supposed to be prophetic of the sorrows in store for the Holy Father.

At times the blood takes the form of black earth, and this appears to denote unworthiness of those who are venerating the relic. One very notable case was that of a priest whose life was far from what the sacred ministry demanded. When he knelt to kiss the reliquary, the blood became very dark. On his departure it regained its natural appearance. Some days after, he fell dead in the midst of a feast.

These extraordinary transformations are witnessed daily by the crowds who flock to the Sanctuary and have been verified and declared authentic by the highest ecclesiastical authorities.

THE MIRACULOUS IMAGE

On the left-hand side of the church and in front of the chapel where the blood of the Martyr is preserved lies the wax figure containing the bones of the Martyr. This rests in a magnificent urn, the front of which consists of a crystal plate, enabling the visitor to see the image distinctly. The figure is clothed in rich robes, and on one of the fingers of the right hand is a massive gold ring, set with a large topaz, which is one of the many gifts sent by St. Pius X to the Saint. The image, like the blood, undergoes extraordinary transformations, which have been witnessed by large numbers of pilgrims and visitors and have been likewise duly authenticated.

The statue in which the bones of the young Martyr are encased was—when it first came from the hands of the artist—far from being a work of art. The figure was uncouth; the face was of a morbid white color; the lips were thick and a grimace was noticeable about the mouth. Unfortunately the ebony case made to contain the statue, a gift of the Bishop of Potenza, was too short, and in consequence the position given to the figure was ungraceful. The case was, notwithstanding, closed and sealed and the key kept in Naples.

The first change noticeable in the statue took place almost immediately after the arrival of the Saint's relics in Mugnano. The 29th of September, 1805, was fixed as the day when the urn was to be placed on the altar prepared for it. To the surprise of all present, extraordinary changes were visible in the statue, though the seals were found to be intact and the key had remained, as we have said, all the time in Naples.

The awkward position given to the statue was changed for one more graceful; the color of the countenance became delicate and bright; and the grimace about the mouth gave place to a pleasing smile. The form of the statue had become elegant. The hair, the hands and the position of the arrows were all changed.

The next great change took place twenty years after: In 1824 the first case was replaced by one more beautiful. The hair had again changed and was more abundant. The eyes opened several times during the public devotions, and when the statue was placed in the new case, which was nearly a foot longer than the former one, the feet, which at first were at some distance from the end, gradually extended themselves so as to touch the extremity of the case.

A new and very striking prodigy occurred in 1841: The statue was so placed that only the profile could be seen by those standing in front. What was not the astonishment of the vast concourse of people when one day the face of the Saint, in the presence of all, turned around, so that fully three-fourths of it became visible.

On the 27th of May, 1892, the statue again changed its position in the presence of a whole pilgrimage, and the change was duly authenticated by the ecclesiastical authorities.

During my own stay in Mugnano, I saw the statue changing color very frequently, passing from pale to a light blush and again to a darker red. The lips were sometimes compressed and sometimes opened. No interference with the statue is possible, since it is placed in the wall and closed in by a thick plate of crystal glass and locked with three keys, which are held by three different authorities. One of these is the Bishop of Nola himself.

THE GREAT STATUE OF THE SAINT

A third object of interest in the sanctuary of the Shrine is a magnificent statue in wood presented by Cardinal Ruffo-Scilla in 1806, which is used in public processions of the Saint. In the year 1823, during the procession, the bearers of the statue felt that it was unusually heavy, and the pilgrims at the same time remarked that the color of the face was much brighter than usual, giving the statue almost a lifelike appearance.

On the following day a kind of sweat, which filled the air with a fragrant perfume, was seen oozing from the forehead and eyes and falling on the breast, where it gathered round the reliquary which rested on the bosom of the Saint. This prodigy lasted a long time and, as in the case of the others, was seen by multitudes of witnesses and duly examined and authenticated by both the ecclesiastical and civil authorities. For these reasons, the statue is naturally held in the highest veneration by the people.

THE SPECIAL SIGN

But the marvel which made the greatest impression on me during my visit was the following: On the ninth day, I was in a side chapel. The Reverend Mother was speaking to a contractor, further up in the church, regarding some repairs. One of the sisters of the Sanctuary approached me and said quite simply:

"Father, have you seen the sign?"

"What sign?" I asked. "I have seen so many wonders during the days I have been here."

"Oh!" she said, "you haven't got *the* sign?"

"If it is anything more wonderful than what I have already seen," I replied, "I would not dare to ask for it. It would be presumption on my part."

"Oh! no, no," she answered. "You have come from a long distance and have remained here so many days; the Little Saint must give you *the sign*."

Saying this, she pulled me gently towards the altar where the urn containing the miraculous image is placed. She had not given me the slightest idea of what this sign consisted of. We knelt in front of the urn and began a short prayer. Suddenly, a sharp report rang out, as if the crystal glass had been struck sharply by something hard. The little sister jumped up, radiant with smiles, and said to me: "Now you have got it." The report was so distinct and sharp that the Reverend Mother, further up in the church, ignorant altogether of what we were about, jumped round and asked, "Whom is it for?"

"It is for the Father," replied the sister.

This knock is a well-known sign given from time to time to clients of the Saint and is, I am happy to say, looked upon as a special mark of her good pleasure. And surely it was a harbinger of good for me.

Arriving in Rome shortly afterwards, I had a private audience with the saintly Pontiff, Pius X, who manifested the greatest pleasure on hearing of my visit to Mugnano and gave me several marks of his favor, one of which was the permission to say a votive mass weekly in honor of the Saint.

THE MULTIPLICATION OF BOOKS

Before closing this chapter, I will mention a last prodigy, namely, the multiplication of books, namely, those of the life of the Saint.

The good priest, Don Francisco di Lucia, who had received the relics, wished to make known the wonders worked by them. For this purpose he wrote a short narrative of the principal events connected with the history of the Saint. This book was being sold rapidly, and the author, wishing to retain some copies for private distribution, sent to Naples for those that remained. They were in all 221. He placed them on the table in five little piles, four of which he covered so as to protect them from the dust. The fifth pile he left uncovered, as the book was in constant demand. For five or six months, he continued to distribute the books freely (to the number of several hundred), always taking them from the uncovered pile, without adverting to the fact that he was taking many more from the pile than it originally contained.

On his return to his house one evening, he was greatly astonished to find the floor of his room, which had been locked, covered with books. As there was no human explanation forthcoming, the good priest thought that it was St. Philomena who had scattered the books as a sign that they were not pleasing to her. However, on examination, he found that of the books on the table, those under cover were just as he had placed them, being forty-five in each group. In the fifth pile, from which he had already taken so many hundreds, quite unconscious that they were being multiplied, there were still nineteen copies left. He now looked over his accounts and found that from this pile he had taken more than 500 books. He next counted the books on the floor and found that they were seventy-two. Other miraculous multiplications took place several times, not only in Mugnano, but in other places as well. These were followed later on by multiplications of the Saint's pictures.

A far different kind of miracle occurred with regard to her relics. Some of those who had received relics did not treat them with sufficient love and respect. What was not their amazement when, on examining their reliquaries, they found that though these were sealed, the relics had disappeared—to be discovered in the urn containing the bones of the Saint when next this was unlocked.

Never have I seen a sanctuary so full of wonders, so alive with the atmosphere of the supernatural, where one sees so palpably heavenly manifestations, as in Mugnano. I do not mean to claim greater things for it than for other sanctuaries, but, as the dear Little Saint's special prerogative seems to consist in her amazing power of miracles and in the extraordinary abundance of favors which she so generously dispenses to her clients, so her sanctuary is especially distinguished for the constant, visible and striking signs which the Almighty is pleased to work in it.

Chapter 6

THE CURÉ OF ARS
AND ST. PHILOMENA

On her return to France from Mugnano, Pauline Jaricot went to visit her dear friend, the venerable Curé of Ars, to whom she recounted the whole history of her miraculous cure. The holy priest, while listening to her with rapt attention, felt a burning love for the Little Saint kindle in his heart. Intense was his joy when Pauline offered him a part of the precious relics which she had brought with her. A chapel was immediately erected in his church in honor of the Virgin Martyr, where the relic was duly placed. This chapel soon became the scene of innumerable cures, conversions and miracles. M. Vianney dedicated himself by special vow to Saint Philomena, and a marvelous intimacy became evident between the good priest and her whom he now considered his Celestial Patroness. He did everything for her, and she did everything for him. She appeared to him, conversed with him and granted everything in answer to his prayers. He called her by the tenderest names, and she delighted in bestowing on him the most wonderful favors. His gift of miracles was extraordinary; yet far from producing in him the slightest notion of vanity, it was the greatest cross he had to bear. He was wont to throw all the "*blame*" on

St. Philomena. "It's St. Philomena. I wish she would work her miracles away from here," he would say with a laugh. But all the same, the Little Saint seemed to take keen pleasure in teasing her holy friend by performing her wonders by his very hands. On one occasion, a poor woman in the midst of a crowded church besought him to bless her sick child. The venerable Curé could not resist the supplications of the poor mother. He blessed the child, and it was instantly restored to health. "Oh! Oh!" said the holy man, full of confusion, making off in haste to the sacristy: "I wish St. Philomena would have cured the child at home."

In season and out of season, he spoke of his "Dear Little Saint." Soon all France rang with her name. Every diocese had altars and chapels and churches dedicated to this Thaumaturga. In Langres alone, there were no less than twelve churches consecrated to her honor. Her three feasts—August 11, her principal festival; May 25, the Finding of her Relics; and the Sunday within the octave of the Ascension, the feast of her Patronage—began to be celebrated with great pomp and attracted immense crowds.

A NEW BOND OF LOVE

Of the many marvels to be seen at Ars during the life of its saintly pastor, none was greater than the daily life of the holy man himself. His frail body was so extenuated with such rigorous fasts and penitential exercises that his emaciated appearance struck the visitors to Ars with awe. Notwithstanding his extreme weakness, the incessant labors which he took on himself each day were enough to exhaust the most herculean strength, were he endowed with it. Day followed day, and crowds thronged to Ars, not only from all parts of France, but from England, Ireland, Germany and the other countries of Europe. The sick, the sorrowful, holy souls as well as the most abandoned sinners, flocked round him, besieging his confessional. They spent long hours, even days, awaiting their turn to pour out their sorrows into his loving heart, or to ask for the solution of some subtle difficulty, or to tell him of the sins and wickedness of a lifetime. One glance from him went straight to the heart of the most hardened reprobate. His angelic smile brought comfort to the most distressed. A word—seemingly inspired—resolved the most intricate doubt. But how he lived! That was *the* miracle of Ars.

DEATH WAS NEAR

At last it seemed that this marvelous life was to end. It was in the beginning of May, 1843. Never had such multitudes been seen in Ars. The servant of God succumbed to the awful fatigue. In addition to the ordinary devotions, it was his wont in the month of May to drag himself from the confessional and mount the pulpit to address the crowds. On the third day this year, he was forced to stop in the middle of his exhortation. In vain he attempted to replace the discourse by the reading of a lecture. He could not continue. Then he tried to recite the usual prayers, but it was in vain. His voice and strength utterly failed him. With difficulty he descended the steps of the pulpit and gained his humble room, where, completely prostrate, he laid himself on the poor couch which served as a bed. Alas! It would seem that the end had come. The doctor from the very first saw that the case was extremely grave. Daily his condition became more alarming, so that on the fifth day the malady had reached an acute stage. Three eminent doctors were called and were obliged to use powerful remedies to check the illness, but it seemed all useless.

Every moment threatened to be the last. Fainting fits and syncopes succeeded each other in rapid succession. The violence of the fever was unabating. No hope remained.

Finally, the danger became so imminent that the Curé's confessor resolved to administer the Last Rites of the Church, which the dying priest received with intense devotion. When asked: "Do you pardon your enemies?" he answered sweetly: "I never wished evil to anyone."

All that night the alarm of the populace was at its height; their venerable Curé was, alas, going to leave them! As the morning brought no improvement, M. Vianney begged that Mass should be offered for him on the altar of his dear Little Saint. Before the Holy Sacrifice commenced, a strange fear seemed to come over him, some extraordinary, terrible anxiety; signs of a most unusual trouble were visible on his countenance. His faithful nurse believed that death was at hand. Scarcely, however, had the Holy Sacrifice begun when the trouble vanished and in an instant he became perfectly calm.

He seemed to have seen something very pleasing, for as Mass ended, he exclaimed to his faithful attendant: "My friend, a great change has come about in me; I am cured!" No doubt his dear Little Saint had appeared to him, for his nurse heard him murmur several times, as if speaking to someone present, the beloved name of Philomena. When someone remarked later in his presence that his cure had been miraculous, he added, "Miraculous—well you may say it." Evidently he had no doubt that he owed his recovery to **Saint Philomena.** His convalescence was rapid. Impatient of restraint, though still extremely weak, he had himself borne to the church where, falling on his knees before the altar of the Blessed Sacrament, he poured forth his soul in acts of burning love and adoration. Then rising up, he made his way to the altar of St. Philomena, where he prayed for a long time with immense joy and consolation. St. Philomena had indeed appeared to him and, in her mysterious colloquy, had revealed to him secrets that were to fill him with joy until his dying day.

CONVERSIONS AT ARS AND WHAT ST. PHILOMENA HAD TO DO WITH THEM

Now more than ever was St. Philomena to work wonders for her holy friend. When great sinners came to him, after exhorting them to sorrow and moving them to repentance, he used to send them to the altar of Saint Philomena to ask her to obtain their conversion. We will quote two of the innumerable instances:

A distinguished savant from Lyons, Monsieur Massiat, set out on a scientific exploration in the mountains. A fellow traveler, an old friend who was going to Ars, said to him: "Come to Ars and I will show you a Curé who works miracles."

"Miracles, my friend!" he said laughing, "I don't believe in miracles."

"Well, come, and I promise that you will see and believe."

"If you could make me believe, that would indeed be a miracle. But as Ars is not far from the scene of my explorations, I don't mind if I do go." The rest of the story we shall leave M. Massiat to tell in his own words:

"Arrived in Ars, my friend put me up at the house of the Widow Gaillard, where we both shared the same room. Early in the morning he called out to me: 'Massiat, will you do me a favor? Will you come to Mass with me?'

" 'Go to Mass? Why, man,' I answered, 'I never went to Mass since my First Communion. Ask me something else.'

" 'You'll come, old friend, just to do me a favor. It is there you can see and judge the Curé for yourself. I only ask you to use your eyes. I will get you a place where you can be at your ease.'

" 'Well, frankly it's not much to my liking,' I replied, 'but I will go simply to please you.'

"We got to the church. My friend put me in the seat facing the sacristy. Shortly afterwards the door opened and the Curé, vested for Mass, made his appearance. His eyes met mine for one instant, but that glance went right to my heart. I felt myself crushed beneath his gaze. I bent my head and covered my face with my hands. All during the Mass, I was immovable. When it ended, I attempted to lift my head and got up to leave the church. Just as I passed the sacristy door, I heard the words, 'Get out, all of you, all out; and a long bony hand rested on my arm, and I felt myself drawn irresistibly into the sacristy, as by an invisible force. The door closed on me. I felt myself again beneath that gaze that seemed to crush me. I blurted out a few confused words: 'Reverend Father, I have a burden on my shoulders that weighs me down.' Then I heard what seemed an angelic voice, such a one as I had never heard before, so sweet that it did not seem to proceed from mortal man.

" 'You must get rid of the burden at once. Go on your knees, tell me your poor life. Our Lord will take the burden, my friend.' Then I commenced my Confession, it was the story of all my life since my First Communion. Little by little, I felt relieved, then consoled, and finally completely at rest. When I had finished, the saintly priest added: 'Come back tomorrow, but now you will go to the altar of St. Philomena and tell her to ask of God your conversion.' I did not weep in the sacristy, but I confess that I wept abundantly at the altar of St. Philomena."

This conversion was one of the most striking that occurred at Ars. M. Massiat lived thenceforth a most fervent life, which was crowned by a most happy death.

The following is the account given by a religious of his own conversion.

"Though reared by a Catholic mother, I soon became a dissolute young vagabond and, after a short absence from home, contracted scandalous vices. My father paid little or no attention to my conduct, but my behavior well-nigh broke my mother's heart. Taking offense at a few words of correction, I resolved to become a soldier, where I foresaw that I could thus better enjoy my liberty. Before I joined my regiment, my mother begged me, with tears in her eyes, as a last

proof of love, to go with her to Ars. I laughed out-
right in her face and scoffed at the idea of going to
Confession. She begged me at least to go to Ars, even
if I did not confess. Her tears and supplications overcame me, and I consented to go, though in anything
but a pleasant frame of mind. But again temptation
awaited me, for on my arrival, I met two of my companions, who sneered at the idea of the Curé's influence. For no other reason than to please my mother,
I went to the church where M. Vianney was teaching
catechism to the children. His appearance struck me
forcibly, and as his eyes met mine, they seemed to see
into the depths of my soul. I began to believe what I
had heard already, that the Curé saw what passed in
the consciences of those who approached him. Yet so
frail is human nature that on meeting my friends after
the lesson, my companions and I enjoyed ourselves
making jokes at the expense of the venerable priest.

"Once more my mother induced me to go to church,
but I was scarcely there than I wished to leave. What
was my amazement when, at that precise moment,
the door of the sacristy opened and the Curé came
straight towards me, making a sign to follow him,
which I did without knowing what I was about! I fell on
my knees and I wept. Seeing me moved, the holy priest
bade me go to the altar of St. Philomena and say five
Our Fathers and Hail Marys. I went. It was the hour
of grace. Something strange happened to me which
I cannot explain. My heart began to beat with such
violence that I was thoroughly frightened. I did not
know how long I remained there. I lost all idea of time.
What I do know is that, in getting up, I was no longer the same man. Tears choked me. I had to go out

and breathe in the open air. My two friends, on seeing me, exclaimed: 'Oh, how you are changed! You have all the appearance of being converted.' 'Perhaps so,' I replied, and turned brusquely on my heels. Though they made most deliberate and wicked attempts to pervert me, thank God I was proof against all temptation and have now been enjoying the bliss of religious life for sixteen years."

It would fill a whole volume, were we to recount all the wonders which St. Philomena worked at the prayers of the dear Curé. Her chapel was a veritable sanctuary of wonders. Thousands came in pilgrimage to ask her intercession. Ex voto offerings of every imaginable type testified to the miracles worked, the favors obtained, the conversions wrought, the blessings granted, the prayers answered. One favor, however, the holy priest asked for in vain, and that was that she would work her miracles someplace else, where people were not likely to attribute them to him. This prayer the Little Saint persistently refused to hear, for she delighted in working her wonders through his instrumentality or in answer to his prayers. With this one exception, a perfect understanding existed between the two, so that the Curé felt her presence, as it were, at his side.

In reply to someone who repeatedly asked him to cure a friend, he replied: "No, no, St. Philomena cured her once. She did not make proper use of it. It's not likely that the Little Saint will do it again." If however, he did not obtain her cure, he obtained for the poor invalid abundant graces, patience, strength and divine consolations.

To a religious who was sent by his superior to solicit the cure of a member of his order whose death would be a great loss to his community M. Vianney replied: "No, no. He is doing much more for his salvation and for his order as he is. He will not be cured."

These were the exceptions. Countless miracles, cures and conversions were the rule.

The venerable Curé of Ars was raised up by God to serve as the model and patron of priests. They are not expected to aspire after his *extraordinary* gifts nor to imitate his *extreme* rigors. That is not possible without a special call from God. But they can easily follow his example in other ways. What can be more easy, for instance, than to imitate his sweet intimacy, his unbounded confidence, his tender devotion to St. Philomena? If priests would only place a statue of this great Thaumaturga in their churches and spread her devotion, as well from the pulpit as in the confessional, their churches would soon become centers of devotion, and abundant graces would flow on pastor and people. The sick, the sorrowful and, above all, the most hardened sinners would soon reap the benefits of the Saint's powerful intercession.

Chapter 7

OTHER FAVORED SANCTUARIES

Pauline Marie Jaricot and the Curé of Ars were the chief instruments used by Divine Providence for spreading the devotion of St. Philomena, not only in France, but in Germany, England, Ireland and the Low Countries. The thousands of visitors who came to Ars learned the devotion from the lips of M. Vianney himself and returned to their respective countries, taking back with them the story of the wonders worked by the Saint.

We will mention a few instances of the rapid growth of the devotion, thus enabling our readers to see how easily they themselves may establish it in their own homes and parishes.

PARIS

In Paris the devotion began very simply. A gentleman who had received a striking favor from St. Philomena offered an image of the Saint to the Church of St. Gervais. This was exposed for the veneration of the faithful, who speedily had reason to recognize in the abundance of favors received the extraordinary power of the new Saint. The cult of the Saint increased so rapidly that in a short time it was found necessary to dedicate one of the side chapels in her honor.

Crowds attended the devotion, and during the novena in preparation for the feast, the church was filled to overflowing by multitudes of the faithful. Many are the stories recounted by the clients of the Saint of the marvels she worked for them. Cures and conversions became frequent; blessings, temporal and spiritual, were received; astounding answers to prayer became so numerous as to cease to cause surprise.

During the time of the Paris Commune (May, 1871), her protection was most especially manifested. The outrages perpetrated in the close vicinity of St. Gervais were some of the most horrible that took place at this awful time. The Communists made several efforts to destroy the church itself but were always foiled in their nefarious attempts. Finally they came in great force under cover of darkness and commenced a thorough sack of the building. All seemed lost when, strange to say, one of their own number hastened for help and drove them out of the sacred edifice.

Though all the buildings in the neighborhood became one vast conflagration, St. Gervais alone stood intact, a silent but eloquent witness to the power of St. Philomena.

Thirteen lamps burn by day and night on the altar, commemorating the thirteen years of the mortal life of the Saint. The oil from these lamps is frequently demanded for use by the sick, and very remarkable indeed are the cures it effects. Each evening a special service is held in honor of the Saint, consisting of prayers, Benediction of the Blessed Sacrament and frequently a panegyric [sermon of praise] on the Saint.

The Archconfraternity of St. Philomena established in the church counts upwards of 8,000 members.

SEMPIGNY

Sempigny in 1830 was a poor parish. The Archbishop of Paris sent a relic of St. Philomena to the church, and this was placed on a wooden altar. A candle which was lighted in honor of the Saint caused a fire, which consumed the entire woodwork of the altar, but seemed to respect the relics. These were untouched by the flames. One of the clients of St. Philomena consoled the poor people of the village at their loss, saying: "She who has already so marvelously shown her power will doubtless provide an altar for herself." And so it came to pass, for shortly after the fire, a young man of ample means read by chance a page torn from the life of the Saint and became so deeply interested in it that he wanted to know all about her. On inquiry, he was informed that she was much honored in Sempigny. Thither he repaired and, while praying before the relic, felt an extraordinary inspiration. It seemed that the holy virgin bade him restore her altar, promising him in return her special protection. The conviction was so vivid that he exclaimed: "I wish for no earthly union, but to take thee, dear Saint, as my sister and my spouse." Whereupon he heard the answer: "Yes, indeed, I will be thy sister and thy spouse, and the Blessed Virgin, my Mother, will be thy Mother also."

He at once set to work and not only restored the altar but the entire church. The Saint on her part showered the most marvelous blessings on her new friend and worked extraordinary prodigies, as well in favor of the people of the district as for the immense crowds of pilgrims who now began to flock to Sempigny from all parts.

THIVET

Thivet is another sanctuary of St. Philomena, and the devotion was introduced there through the instrumentality of a young man. He was grievously ill and was despaired of by the doctors, who gave him up for lost. Unable to make the journey himself, he begged a good priest to go to Ars and solicit his cure. His envoy accordingly set out and said Mass at the altar of St. Philomena, after which he repaired to the tomb of the holy Curé, who had died a short time previously. There he heard a voice, as if issuing from the tomb, telling him that the sick man would be cured if St. Philomena were honored in the neighborhood where he lived. So startling was the impression that the priest turned cold and began to tremble in every limb. This impression, far from lessening, became more intense. Accepting the compact, he speedily set about establishing the devotion, having obtained a relic of the Saint from Miss Jaricot. Shortly afterwards, the patient was perfectly restored to health and in company with his priest-friend made a pilgrimage to Ars to thank St. Philomena. Just as in other places where her devotion was introduced, favors, blessings, graces of all kinds began to be showered on the people. An association in the Saint's name was established, which included in a short time thousands of members from all over France.

Let not our readers imagine that the instances we have given are exceptional; they are rather the rule.

The advent of the Saint to a church or district is the signal for the most amazing blessings.

The wonders wrought in some of the sanctuaries of St. Philomena are so marvelous as almost to rival those of Mugnano itself.

Would only that priests could be induced to place a statue of the Saint in their churches. She herself would do the rest.

Chapter 8

THE SOVEREIGN PONTIFFS
AND ST. PHILOMENA

At the beginning of the 19th century, St. Philomena was utterly unknown to the Church and to the world. No mention of her name or martyrdom had come down in tradition, nor do we find the slightest trace of her history in the acts of the martyrs. Yet before the century had closed, her name resounded through the length and breadth of Christendom. Cardinals, patriarchs, archbishops and bishops, generals of religious orders, members of the secular clergy, men eminent for sanctity, kings, too, and princes, nobles and plebeians flocked in crowds to the humble village of Mugnano to pray at the feet of this wonder-working Saint. The prodigies she worked were so marvelous as almost to defy belief. Her fame spread throughout Italy, thence to France and all the countries in Europe. It crossed the ocean, and in a short time her sanctuaries and shrines were to be found in America, Australia, China and Japan, and always with the same results. Whenever a picture of her or a statue was exposed, whether in private houses or in public churches, there cures and wonders, graces and blessings were showered on her clients.

WHAT THE POPES THINK OF
ST. PHILOMENA

However, what seems to be the most significant feature in the devotions to our Saint is that, ever since the finding of her relics, Pope after Pope, not content with lavishing honors on her, has one after the other cherished a particular and tender personal devotion to the wonder-working Little Saint.

When the sarcophagus containing her relics was discovered in the Catacombs, the usual rigorous precautions ordained by the *Ritual* were stringently enforced, with the object of securing the greatest possible accuracy and preventing the smallest danger of error in all that concerned the newly discovered heroine of the Faith.

The astounding and constant prodigies which were worked through her intercession attracted universal attention and focused all eyes on the Thaumaturga, while at the same time they aroused the bitter hostility and called forth the scathing sarcasm of sceptics and unbelievers. But in the wonderful ways of God, this adverse criticism eventually redounded to the greater glory of St. Philomena, for it caused the ecclesiastical tribunals to be still more vigilant in accepting and examining the various facts alleged in favor of or contrary to the devotion. As a result of the increased vigilance, an absolute guarantee was secured of the genuineness of all that had been recounted of the Saint. It is eminently consoling that, of all the tributes paid to her, the most touching and eulogistic have come from the Sovereign Pontiffs themselves.

Leo XII, over and over again, expressed the highest admiration for the extraordinary power conferred by the Almighty on this hitherto unknown child Saint and listened with delight to the accounts given him of the wonders she worked. So authentic did he account the information he received and so irrefutable the facts related to him that, notwithstanding the extreme care which the Church usually takes in such matters, he had no hesitation in allowing altars to be dedicated and chapels to be erected in her honor.

Gregory XVI was himself a witness of the great miracle of Mugnano, the cure of Pauline Marie Jaricot. He visited her in Rome before her departure for Mugnano and verified for himself the desperate condition in which she lay. On her return to Rome Miss Jaricot was received by the Sovereign Pontiff with the warmest affection. He did not conceal his amazement, exclaiming: "Is this, indeed, our daughter, or is it a vision from the other world?"

Though profoundly touched by what he himself declared to be "a miracle of the first class," he in nowise relaxed the rigorous laws of the Roman tribunals. On the contrary, he commanded the Sacred Congregation of Rites to proceed at once to a thorough investigation of the cause. The difficulties that had arisen were carefully analyzed; the doubts that had been raised were sifted to the utmost. All the facts—from the discovery of the relics in 1802 to the latest miracles worked by the Saint—were subjected to the minutest scrutiny, and this by the most experienced and keenest experts in Rome. After a protracted examination, the Sacred

Congregation gave a full and favorable decision in favor of the cult of the Saint. Yet the Holy Father, notwithstanding his own personal love for St. Philomena, spent two more years in prayer and deliberation before making his final pronouncement.

At last, to the great delight of the Saint's devoted clients, among whom were numbered several distinguished bishops, archbishops and cardinals, the solemn approval of the Church was made public. This was so complete and conferred so much glory on the Saint that it most amply compensated for the delay which had occurred.

The Pope was not content that St. Philomena should be raised to the honors of the altar and that her feast be established and her office given to the Church; he went much further and declared her to be "**the Great Wonder-Worker of the XIXth Century**," thus giving the Church's solemn sanction to those marvelous prodigies alleged to have been worked by the Saint and effectually silencing the self-constituted critics who had taken on themselves to ridicule her cult in the face of overwhelming evidence.

Not long after, the same Holy Father gave the Saint the new title of "**Patroness of the Living Rosary.**"

As a last act of devotion and with the object of manifesting his personal affection for the Holy Virgin, the Pontiff sent a magnificent gold and silver lamp to her Sanctuary in Mugnano.

Pius IX was perhaps of all the Popes the one who showed most special devotion to the Saint. When Archbishop of Spoleto he was already her devout client and earnestly spread her devotion. Later on, when Archbishop of Imola, he fell dangerously ill, and the greatest fears were entertained for his life. Near his bedside stood a beautiful image of his dear Saint, who was heard to rap distinctly, as she sometimes does when about to perform some great miracle. Immediately, favorable symptoms were noticed in the patient, and these speedily developed into rapid convalescence. Years rolled by, and the Archbishop became the immortal Pontiff, Pius IX, of Papal Infallibility and the Immaculate Conception fame.

Far from forgetting his dear Patroness when raised to the throne of St. Peter, this great Pope availed himself of his supreme power to shed still greater luster on the name of St. Philomena.

To the intense joy of the inhabitants of Mugnano, he went on a pilgrimage to the Shrine of his benefactress, where he was solemnly received by the Bishop of Nola, the King, Queen and all the members of the Royal Family of Naples. He said Mass on the altar of the Saint and afterwards publicly venerated her relics. He also declared her to be the secondary **"Patroness of the Kingdom of Naples."** In the year 1849 he named St. Philomena **"Patroness of the Children of Mary."**

He granted her, later on, a proper office, which is such an extraordinary privilege that rarely or never has it been granted to any other Saint under similar circumstances.

When dying, the aged Pontiff sent a most beautiful offering to Mugnano, the last touching tribute of his love and gratitude.

Leo XIII, before becoming Pope, made two pilgrimages to Mugnano. Later on, when Vicar of Christ, he sent a valuable cross to the Sanctuary. He approved the Confraternity of the Saint and raised it to the rank of an Archconfraternity, enriching it with important indulgences.

Pius X was no less devout to the Little Saint, to whom he sent by special envoy a magnificent gold ring and other costly presents. He was always pleased to hear of the wonders she worked, as the writer himself knows by experience, for in a private audience which it was his great privilege to have with the Pope, the Holy Father spoke most affectionately of the Little Saint.

When the seal of God's infallible Church is placed on a devotion and when Christ's Vicar on earth gives it his own solemn approbation, it becomes at once worthy of our profoundest respect and reverence. What then must be thought of a devotion that Pope after Pope has not only sanctified by his supreme authority, but recommended by his own personal example and love? Surely nothing is more consoling for the clients of St. Philomena than that the Vicars of Christ themselves should so clearly manifest their belief in her wonder-working powers of intercession.

Chapter 9

THE INTERCESSION OF THE SAINTS

The leading feature in the history of St. Philomena, that which in fact constitutes her special characteristic, is the extraordinary power conferred on her by God of working wonders. This it was that won for her from the Popes the glorious title of "The Wonder-Worker of the XIX Century." It will therefore not be amiss if in the present sketch we give a few explanations which may help our readers to a better understanding of the marvels recounted in the lives of so many great Saints.

The generality of Christians, grounded as they are in the Faith, readily acknowledge the wonders wrought by God's faithful servants. Carping critics, however, within and without the Fold, profess to find difficulty in accepting such facts.

SECONDARY CAUSES

The first query that we are confronted with is this: Why have recourse to the Saints? Why not go directly to God Himself? He is the all-merciful and bountiful Father and Lord of all. His Saints are neither as good nor as bountiful as He.

The answer is not far to seek: The Almighty bestows on us His favors *directly* when it so pleases Him. In His all-wise Providence, however, He frequently chooses to bestow His graces through the hands of His Blessed Mother and by the ministrations of His Angels and Saints, in other words, through secondary causes. We therefore pray to the Saints by His express wish and determination.

In the Old Dispensation we read how the Prophet Eliseus cured Naaman the leper not immediately by any word or act of his own, but by ordering him to bathe seven times in the waters of the Jordan. The Patriarchs and Prophets frequently made intercession for Israel, and through them God gave His favors to His chosen People. Priests were appointed to offer sacrifices; Moses and Jeremias acted as mediators; Isaac and Jacob called down blessings on their sons and descendants.

When on earth, Jesus Christ Himself, the Son of God, anointed with a mixture of clay and spittle the blind man's eyes and so gave him back his sight. And again we read how He bade the lepers show themselves to the priests, and on the way they were cured. He might, if He so willed, have given sight to the blind man by a single word. But He chose to use clay mixed with spittle as an instrument. He might have said to the lepers: "I wish, be you clean." His will was otherwise.

In the use of the Sacraments, the same doctrine is exemplified. The new-born babe is purified by the Baptism of water. Men's sins are forgiven through the instrumentality of priests in Confession. All the Sacraments are visible signs and instruments through which graces are conferred.

In like manner, God is pleased very frequently to bestow His favors through the intercession of His

Saints, and it is not easy to see how any thoughtful Christian can have difficulty in understanding a matter in itself so plain. Which of us objects to accepting a blessing from an aged father or refuses a prayer from a kind friend, though these be men and women like ourselves? If we can believe that frail mortals, still in the flesh, can by their blessings and prayers do us good, much more credible is it that God's intimate friends, who enjoy the sunshine of His presence and the intimacy of His blessed friendship, can win for us favors and graces.

The Saints whose intercession we invoke are servants of God renowned for remarkable sanctity and purity of life, and the Church rightly teaches that these great friends of God can, by their prayers and merits, obtain for us graces which we should not otherwise receive.

ANOTHER DIFFICULTY

Granted the wisdom of the Church in allowing us to have recourse to the Saints, we must, however (say our critics), have some recognized rule. We cannot be expected to believe every story we hear, nor accept extraordinary facts on the mere authority of some extravagant devotee. Daily we hear people use such expressions as, "He is a Saint," or, "That is a miracle." Surely no intelligent man can be called on to endorse such arbitrary decisions.

Our nervous brethren profess to fear exaggeration, false enthusiasm and dangerous novelties. So do we, and much more so does Holy Church. But the solemn assurance of the Sovereign Pontiffs surely ought to be sufficient to allay such fears. When we come to understand what precautions the Church takes concerning all that has to do with the Saints, our vain doubts soon disappear. A few explanations will help our readers to judge for themselves.

THE CANONIZATION OF SAINTS

The procedure of the Roman Congregations regarding the cult of the Saints is so rigorous that we find no parallel for it in human tribunals.

Any indiscreet efforts on the part of friends, no matter how well-intentioned these may be, to push the cause of a Saint, far from helping the process, are likely to be seriously detrimental to it. Interference of this kind may defer for long years, or even cause to be put aside altogether, the canonization in question. The Church's sole desire is to know the will of Heaven and she is, in consequence, most solicitous to exclude the collusion of any human agency in a matter so sacred.

Therefore, before the cause of a Saint is introduced, long years are allowed to pass in order that all partisan enthusiasm may subside. The continuation of the cult during these long years, when all human sympathies, associations and memories are completely severed, implies an intervention of Providence to keep alive the devotion, and it is interpreted as such by the Church.

Information on the life of the Saint is gathered in the meantime with the minutest care. This is then sifted so carefully that not the smallest flaw can pass undetected, and it must be proved that the Saint in question was not only eminent for sanctity, but had practiced *heroic* virtue.

Miracles are the next essential. These in turn are

subjected to the keenest scrutiny. The facts alleged must allow of no possible doubt, and they must be testified to by witnesses of unimpeachable confidence. Their miraculous character, above all, must be beyond all possible suspicion.

Lastly, one of the ablest and most experienced of Roman theologians is appointed to search into the cause and discover any possible weakness which there may be connected with it. The difficulties he raises have to be fully answered, the doubts he puts forward perfectly solved before the cause can proceed. He is, to a certain extent, what the Crown Prosecutor is in our [British] courts, but his cross examination is far more subtle and far-reaching. In popular parlance, he is called the "Devil's Advocate," for he is the legal opposer of the canonization of the Saint, and it is his obligation to do all in his power to find reasons to prevent it. His real title is *Promotor Fidei*, "Promotor of the Faith." Causes without number have been brought to a standstill at this stage, owing to the difficulty in solving the doubts raised by this subtle investigator.

THE CHURCH'S CAUTION

It has been remarked with great reason that the fact of being canonized is in itself a miracle, for what might appear a trivial difficulty to the uninitiated is sufficient in the mind of the Church to put back the cause for years, or even centuries.

St. Margaret Mary, great Saint though she was, died in the year 1690 and was canonized only in 1919. St. Joan of Arc died in 1481, and only after the lapse of five centuries was she raised to the honors of the altar.

Others there are—though indeed very few—whose cause the Church permits to proceed more rapidly. This does not imply less care, but only that the proofs are more abundant and evident, and the Church, interpreting the designs of Providence, hastens the deliberations of her tribunals.

Saint Thérèse of Lisieux is a case in point. She was born, died, and was canonized in our own days. St. Peter Martyr, the great Dominican Saint, was canonized a year after his death. The mother of Saint Aloysius Gonzaga assisted at his beatification, but he was not canonized until centuries later.

Only when the Pope and the Sacred Congregation, consisting of the most learned and venerable theologians, declare themselves *perfectly* satisfied, is the Saint beatified or canonized and the faithful invited to venerate him and invoke his intercession.

Then indeed, when in answer to fervent supplications the prayers of the people are heard and striking favors are accorded, the faithful are within their right piously to believe that these blessings were vouchsafed through the merits of the Saint whom they so confidently invoked. When hundreds and thousands of the faithful address their supplications to the Saint and are likewise heard in a very special way, the Saint naturally becomes what is known as a popular Saint, and his intercession is more constantly implored.

We must bear in mind that the faithful never arrogate to themselves the right to declare one fact or another a *miracle*; the Church reserves that decision to herself. If some ignorant Catholics from mistaken zeal behave imprudently or use the word *miracle* improperly, their action in nowise militates against the wisdom of invoking the Saints. Much more to be deplored is the flippant criticism of those who, for light or imaginary reasons, scoff at the testimony of competent witnesses and constitute themselves judges of what they so little understand.

POPULAR SAINTS

A careful perusal of Church history shows us that in all ages God has raised up in His Church special Saints to whom He grants special power to distribute His graces in a special way. All the world over, the faithful with simple faith pray to St. Anthony if something is lost. People are never tired of telling the wonderful things he does. St. Vincent Ferrer, of the Dominican Order, was perhaps the greatest wonder-worker the Church has ever known. He sounded his miracle bell daily to summon the deaf, the dumb, the paralytic, the maimed to be cured, nay, he even gave to others the power of working miracles.

Moreover, the Church is accustomed to appoint patron Saints whose aid we are counselled to solicit in dangers and temptations. St. Thomas Aquinas is Patron of Purity, St. Aloysius Gonzaga is Patron of Youth, Bl. Imelda is Patroness of First Communicants, St. Philomena is Patroness of the Children of Mary. St. Christopher was recently named Protector of Motorists, St. Bernard of Menthon of Mountain Climbers.

SUCH STRANGE STORIES

In the case of St. Philomena, the great stone of scandal would seem to be that the favors accorded by her

are so wonderful, so frequent, so universal that sceptics seem to think that "it is all too good to be true"
and conclude by some new process of reasoning that,
because they are so frequent and wonderful, they must
therefore be spurious!

In answer to this strange objection much can be said!
First of all, we will quote no less an authority than St.
Thomas Aquinas for the reasonableness of believing in
pious narratives. This great light of the Church, distinguished as much for his consummate prudence as for
his angelic intelligence, read daily and with the greatest avidity the *Lives of the Fathers of the Desert* by Cassian.
So did St. Dominic and very many other great Saints
before him. Now this book contains very wonderful
stories of the hermits and Saints of the early Church,
and so quaint are these recitals, so at variance with
the world's way of thinking, that nothing recounted
of St. Philomena exceeds them in strangeness. Yet in
the reading of these stories the Angelic Doctor [St.
Thomas Aquinas] found the choicest food for medita-
tion, derived from them his deepest consolation and
considered them a most powerful stimulus to sanctity.

No one will dare to suggest that the Angelic Doctor,
the Prince of Theologians, the Light of the Church,
the wisest of the Saints, was guilty of indiscretion or
accepted lightly mere foolish legends. If he who was
constantly rapt in the sublimest contemplation found
time, nay, considered it an obligation to peruse these
gracious stories, it was because he accepted them with
faith and found in them a powerful aid to sanctity.

The hagiologies [biographies of the Saints] of the
great religious orders furnish us with an endless series
of equally touching narrations, which have been the

delight of the greatest Saints and the most eminent theologians of the Church. Our critics, applying their false criteria to these, condemn and ridicule them with the same asperity, the same foolish temerity, the same supercilious arrogance with which they scoff at the wonders recounted of St. Philomena.

If we open the Old Testament, we find in it facts and happenings very similar to those which provoke the scorn of our sceptics. These, however, are SACRED SCRIPTURE, which at least no Catholic may reject. Our contention is that if God in the Old Law—which was a Law of fear and infinitely removed from the loving condescension of the New Dispensation —vouchsafed to grant such proofs of love and intimacy to His chosen people, surely it is not more wonderful that in the plenitude of His love and mercy toward mankind, which is the New Law and in which we now live, His bounty be equally large, His measure equally generous.

"Such strange things are told of her!" Yes, and it was for that very reason that Pope Gregory XVI always referred to her as the "Great Wonder-Worker of the XIXth century." The Acts of the Martyrs abound in the most amazing prodigies that no sane man could deny. They were worked in the Roman amphitheatre, before multitudes of pagan spectators, who were so convinced by them that thousands were converted, enduring in consequence the most cruel torments in defense of their newborn faith. If these holy martyrs, while still in the flesh, could command such signs, why deny the power to one of their number now in Heaven?

But are we bound to believe all the stories we hear of St. Philomena? Certainly not! But we are bound not to scoff at the devotion of others with whose conduct and consciences we have no right to interfere. They are quite as good judges of the matter as we, and it is not too much to ask of us to reverence the decision and respect the example of the Roman Pontiffs who approved her cult, declared authentic the wonders attributed to her and cherished for her most fervent personal devotion.

While not *bound* to believe all that is recounted by the pious clients of the Saint, we would do well to discriminate a little. Thereby we shall find abundant evidence to prove the genuineness of innumerable of these miracles, which countless multitudes of the faithful, as well as learned theologians, saintly bishops, and the Roman Pontiffs themselves consider authentic. Facts are stubborn arguments, and it is a well-authenticated fact that from the moment the relics of St. Philomena were discovered in the Catacombs, the most stupendous miracles were worked by their means, not in one place or other, but all the world over! It is equally certain that not only at her shrine at Mugnano, but wherever she has been invoked, the Saint continues to work the same astounding prodigies. This series of wonders has now been going on since 1805, when the relics were transferred to Mugnano, a period of almost two hundred years! It would be rash to cast doubt on such solid and cumulative evidence, as it would also be superlatively foolish for any of us to imagine that he has discovered flaws that have escaped the keen vigilance of the Roman authorities.

It was only natural that, on the finding of the relics which had lain hidden for seventeen centuries in the Catacombs, difficulties arose which demanded explanation. This was given in the most scholarly way by eminent archeologists. Since then Pope after Pope, as we have seen, has manifested devotion to St. Philomena, and the most enlightened servants of God have been most devoted to her, not only the saintly Curé of Ars, but also a host of others, such as St. Mother Sophie Barat; M. Leo Dupont (the "Holy Man of Tours"); St. Peter Julian Eymard, founder of the Priests of the Most Blessed Sacrament; St. Peter Chanel; Madame de Bonnault d'Honet, foundress of the Faithful Companions of Jesus—all, distinguished for sanctity or eminent piety, have been fervent clients of St. Philomena.

We can afford, therefore, to pursue our devotion to the dear Little Saint with tranquil minds.

Chapter 10

WHO WAS ST. PHILOMENA?

Despite many learned investigations, nothing has been discovered to throw light on the personal history of St. Philomena previous to the finding of her relics in the Catacombs. Some of her ardent clients, however, emboldened by the sweet graciousness with which the dear Little Saint is accustomed to hear the prayers of her servants, besought her earnestly to make known to them who she was and what she suffered for Jesus Christ. Their prayers were heard, and the Saint revealed to three different people, living far apart and utterly unknown to each other, the story of her life and the details of her martyrdom.

These revelations, though of a private character, are nevertheless striking and carry with them no small weight of human probability. The fact that they were made to three persons, that these were unknown to each other, and yet that the revelations were identical, is, to say the least of it, a very extraordinary coincidence.

Moreover, they tally admirably with what we know of the Saint, being perfectly in keeping with the writing and symbols that were found on the sarcophagus.

Lastly, the revelations have been frequently published and the book containing them received the Imprimatur of the Holy Office on December 21, 1833.

This does not imply that the Holy See guarantees the authenticity of the revelations—that it rarely does in the case of private revelations—but it shows that we are within our right in accepting them on their own merits and that the Church finds nothing in them worthy of censure.

As our readers will doubtless be anxious to know all that there is to be known concerning our Saint, we shall quote one of the three revelations, namely, that made to Mother Mary Louisa, Superior General of the Congregation of the Dolours of Mary, who died in the odor of sanctity in the year 1875.

ST. PHILOMENA'S STORY

"My dear Sister," the Saint revealed to her, "I was the daughter of the king of a small Grecian state. My mother too was of royal blood. As they had no children, my parents continually offered sacrifices and prayers to their false gods to obtain the blessing of a child. There was at that time with our family a Roman doctor named Publius, now a Saint in Heaven, though he did not suffer martyrdom. Touched by their blindness and moved by their sorrow, he was inspired by the Holy Ghost to speak to them of our faith and assured them that their prayers would be heard if they embraced the Christian Religion. His fervid eloquence touched their hearts, and their minds were at the same time enlightened by divine grace. After mature deliberation, they finally received the holy Sacrament of Baptism.

"I was born at the beginning of the following year, on January 10th, and was called 'Lumena' or 'Light,' as I had been born in the light of the Faith, to which my parents were now ardently devoted. They gave me the name of 'Philomena' at Baptism, that is, 'Friend of the Light' which illumined my soul by the grace of this Sacrament. Divine Providence permitted that the epitaph on my sarcophagus should be explained in this very sense, though the interpreters were not aware that it was the exact thought in the minds of those who had originally written it.

"My parents lavished every affection on me, and my father could not bear to have me out of his sight. For this reason, I accompanied them to Rome at the close of my thirteenth year. This journey was undertaken in consequence of the declaration of war unjustly made on us by the proud and powerful Roman Emperor. Realizing his weakness, my poor father started for Rome in the hopes of making peace with the Emperor. My mother and myself went with him and were present at the audience he had with the tyrant.

"How wonderful is destiny! Who should have guessed mine? While my father earnestly pleaded his cause and sought to justify himself, the Emperor kept glancing at me and replied: 'Do not trouble yourself further; you may be perfectly at rest; there is no cause for anxiety. Instead of attacking you, I will place the forces of the Empire at your disposal on condition that you give me the hand of your fair daughter Philomena in marriage.' My parents agreed to his request, and on our return home sought to convince me that I should be, indeed, happy as Empress of Rome. I rejected the offer without a moment's hesitation and told them that I had made myself the spouse of Jesus Christ by a vow of chastity when I was eleven years old.

"My father then endeavored to prove that a child of

my age could not dispose of herself as she pleased and exerted all his authority to force me to obey. My Divine Spouse, however, gave me the necessary strength to stand by my resolution.

"When the Emperor was acquainted with my answer, he regarded it merely as a pretext for breaking faith with him. 'Bring the Princess Philomena here,' he said to my father, 'and I will see if I cannot persuade her.'

"My father came for me, but seeing that my resolution was unshaken, both he and my mother, casting themselves at my feet, implored me to change my mind. 'O daughter!' they exclaimed, 'Have pity on your parents! Have pity on your country! Have pity on our Kingdom!' I answered that my virginity must take precedence of all else.

"Nevertheless, we had to obey the Emperor and present ourselves at the Palace. At first he used promises and blandishments of all kinds to induce me to accept marriage, but all in vain. He then had recourse to threats, but with no better result. At last, in a fit of fury, inspired by the demon of impurity, he ordered me to be thrown into a dungeon beneath the Imperial Palace. Here I was bound hand and foot and loaded with chains in the hope of compelling me to agree to marry this man in whose soul the spirit of evil alone held sway.

"Daily, the Emperor came in person to renew his attentions. He had the irons removed so that I could take a little bread and water, but seeing that his efforts were in vain, he would renew my torments. All this time, my Divine Spouse supported me. I recommended myself unceasingly to Jesus and to His Blessed Mother.

"These scenes had lasted for thirty-seven days when

the Queen of Heaven appeared to me surrounded by a dazzling light and bearing her Divine Son in her arms. 'My child,' she said, 'you will remain three more days in this dungeon and then, on the fortieth day of your imprisonment, you will leave this place of sorrow.'

"On hearing these words of comfort, my heart beat for joy.

" 'When leaving it,' continued the Blessed Mother of God, 'you will undergo cruel torture for the love of my Son.'

"These new tidings filled me with fear, and I felt as it were all the bitter agony of dying.

" 'Courage, beloved daughter,' added the Queen of Heaven, 'beloved above all others, for you bear my name and the name of my Son. You are called Lumena or Light. My Son, your Spouse, is called Light, Star, Sun. And am I not likewise called Dawn, Star, Moon, Sun? I will be your support. Now is the hour of human weakness and humiliation, but when the moment of trial arrives, you will receive strength and grace. Besides your Angel Guardian, you will have at your side the Archangel Gabriel, whose name signifies, 'The strength of the Lord.' When I was on earth he was my protector. I will now send him to her who is my beloved daughter.' These reassuring words restored my courage, and when the vision disappeared, a refreshing perfume remained in the dungeon.

"The Emperor, despairing of inducing me to accede to his desires, had recourse to torture in order to terrify me and induce me to break my vow to Heaven. He ordered me to be tied to a pillar and scourged mercilessly, to the accompaniment of horrible blasphemies.

" 'Since she is so obstinate as to prefer a malefactor

condemned to death by his own countrymen to an emperor like me,' he said, 'she deserves condign [fitting] punishment.'

"The tyrant, seeing that though I was one gaping wound, my determination was unaltered, ordered me to be brought back to prison to die in agony. I was looking forward to death to fly to the bosom of my Spouse when two bright angels appeared and poured a heavenly balm on my wounds. I was cured. The following morning the Emperor was astounded on hearing the news. Seeing me stronger and more beautiful than ever, he endeavored to persuade me that I owed this favor to Jupiter, who destined me for the imperial diadem.

"The Holy Ghost inspiring me, I rejected his sophistry and resisted his caresses. Mad with rage, he gave orders that an iron anchor should be attached to my neck and that I should be thrown into the Tiber. But Jesus, to show His power and confound the false gods, once more sent His two angels to help me. They cut the cord, and the anchor fell to the bottom of the river, where it remained embedded in the mud. They then brought me back to the bank without a single drop of water having touched my garments.

"This miracle converted several of the bystanders. Diocletian, more obstinately blind than Pharaoh, now declared that I must be a witch and ordered me to be pierced with arrows. Mortally wounded and on the point of death, I was once more cast into prison. Instead of death, which should naturally have been mine, the Almighty sent a peaceful sleep, after which I awoke more beautiful than before. On hearing of this new miracle, the Emperor was so infuriated that he ordered the torture to be repeated until death should supervene, but the arrows refused to leave the bows. Diocletian insisted that this was the result of magic, and hoping that witchcraft would be unavailing against fire, he gave orders that the arrows should be heated red-hot in a fiery furnace. This precaution was of no avail. My Divine Spouse saved me from the torture by turning the arrows back on the archers, six of whom were killed. This last miracle brought about other conversions, and the people began to show serious signs of disaffection towards the Emperor and even reverence for our Holy Faith.

"Fearing more serious consequences, the tyrant now ordered me to be beheaded. My soul, glorious and triumphant, ascended into Heaven, there to receive the crown of virginity which I had merited by so many victories. It was three o'clock in the afternoon of the 10th of August, which was a Friday.

"Behold the reasons why Our Lord willed that my body should be brought back to Mugnano on August 10th and why He worked such miracles on that occasion."[1]

---

1 St. Philomena's feast day was at first observed on August 10, but the Church changed it to August 11 out of respect for St. Lawrence, whose feast is August 10.—*Editor*, 1993.

Chapter 11

HOW TO HONOR ST. PHILOMENA

HER CORD

From the very beginning of the devotion to St. Philomena, the use of her cord was one of the many ways by which the Saint was honored and her protection secured. We know for instance that the holy Curé of Ars blessed and distributed them himself. The Confraternity of the Cord of St. Philomena is now approved of by the Congregation of Rites and is enriched with many indulgences.

The cord is white and red and may be made of either linen, wool or cotton threads so interwoven as to give an almost equal preponderance to the two colors, the one representing virginity, the other martyrdom.

The use of the cord has become very popular, for it has been the means of working innumerable miracles and obtaining thousands of cures. It is used by the sick, by those in tribulation, by those who are fighting against temptations—and always with the most amazing results. It is a protection against evils and accidents of every kind. The formula of blessing the cord is that found in the *Roman Ritual.* Attestations like the following are innumerable.

The Superioress of a well-known convent affirms:

"St. Philomena is just a wonder. For the past four years I have given her cord to a great number of sick, including some members of our own community. All were cured, excepting two or possibly three, and in these few cases it indeed seemed clear that the best thing for them was to go to our good God."

The Mother Superior of the Reparation Convent in C . . . : "For years back I have had recourse to St. Philomena in all my needs. I was myself threatened with a most serious operation, but I put on the cord, and thank God, there was no further need of an operation. Now I go to her for everything."

A young lady declares: "My confidence in St. Philomena is intense. I never fail to recommend her devotion. I was grievously ill and put on her cord, which restored me to health."

A priest declares: "I was very ill and had great reason to fear the gravest consequences. I put on the cord of St. Philomena and promised to promote devotion to her. It was enough; I was able to get up the same day."

From a nun: "One of our children fell dangerously ill and was threatened with the gravest complications. We put the cord of St. Philomena on the little sufferer, who experienced immediate relief, and in a few hours all danger had passed."

Children who have been girded with the blessed cord of the Virgin Martyr have, in those countless mishaps and accidents which are so frequent in the case of the young, been most marvelously preserved from harm. Mothers would do well to see that their little ones wear this blessed cord. What dangers would they not escape!

These are a few of the thousands of cases that we

could quote, but they are sufficient to show the extraordinary efficacy of the devotion.

THE OIL OF SAINT PHILOMENA

The oil that has been used in the lamps burning before the statue of St. Philomena is very frequently used by the sick, as we have seen in the case of St. Gervais, Paris. Some anoint their eyes and have their sight restored; some their limbs, which are strengthened; some their ears, which recover their hearing. The oil taken from any lamp burned before St. Philomena's statue may be used.

CHAPLET OF ST. PHILOMENA

The little Chaplet of St. Philomena consists of white beads, a token of virginity, red beads, the sign of martyrdom, and a St. Philomena medal. There are three white beads in honor of the Blessed Trinity, in whose honor the holy virgin laid down her life. The red beads are thirteen in number and signify the thirteen years that St. Philomena lived on earth. This little Chaplet is one of the simplest ways of praying to the Saint. (See pp. 173-174 for prayers.)[1] When saying it, we may very properly ask, firstly, for the grace of purity, in honor of the virginity of the Saint, who sacrificed life and honor in defense of this angelic virtue. Secondly, we should do well to ask for the strength and courage ever to do our duty, a virtue for which she was so eminently

---

1 For sources of St. Philomena devotional items, see the last pages of this book.—*Editor*, 1993.

distinguished and which she is so ready to obtain for all her devoted clients.

This great grace alone helps a Christian to arrive at the highest sanctity, in the most practical and easy way.

NOVENAS

A novena to St. Philomena may be made by saying the beautiful Litany of St. Philomena, or some other prayer to the Saint (see p. 171 ff.), for nine days in succession. When the intention is very important, it is well to assist at Mass and receive Communion during nine days.

Marvelous results, too, are obtained by having a novena of Masses said in her Sanctuary at Mugnano.[2]

MEDALS

Many clients of the Saint place great confidence in the use of her blessed medals. These are easily obtained and are very pretty. Like every other object used in connection with the Saint, they are of the greatest efficacy. They have the special advantage of being easily used and may be carried in one's pocket or attached to one's beads.

PICTURES OF ST. PHILOMENA

Great graces have been obtained by venerating the Saint's pictures. These may be placed in the living

---

2 The address is: Sanctuary of St. Philomena, 83027 Mugnano del Cardinale (Avellino), Italy.

room or in bedrooms. Many favors have been granted to those who keep a lamp burning before the picture, even though this be lighted only one day in the week. It is well to place these pictures near the sick and suggest to them the extraordinary advantages of praying with confidence to this great Saint, whose power has been very specially manifested in favor of the sick and infirm. Countless cures are being daily granted in answer to the simple but confident prayers of her devout clients.

We can suggest nothing more calculated to please the Saint and secure her powerful protection than the offering of a picture or statue to some church or convent where a center of devotion to her may be thus established. Many of her great sanctuaries have had this simple beginning.

SPREADING DEVOTION TO
ST. PHILOMENA

Another very efficacious method of winning the love and friendship of the "Dear Little Saint" is by spreading her devotion and making her wonder-working power known far and wide.

The easiest way of attaining this end is by distributing the Life or History of the Saint to as large a number of people as possible. It is almost impossible to peruse the simple narrative of all the wonders she works and the favors she obtains without feeling a powerful attraction and a warm affection for the dear Thaumaturga. Those who spread her devotion may rest assured of her powerful protection.

A REMARKABLE RESCUE

The following story comes to us from Italy. It will show how efficacious is any object worn in honor of the Saint.

A beautiful statue of the Saint arrived in the town. Among those who gathered to see the image was a ragged little boy, who snatched a bit of paper in which the statue had been wrapped and hid it in his breast as a relic of Saint Philomena. Some days later, he fell into a deep well, where he remained for a considerable time. On falling into the well, the little fellow called on St. Philomena. The Virgin Martyr appeared and pulled him out of the water, took him in her arms and held him up.

His companions ran for help, which only arrived after fully an hour. A rope was then let down and the lad cried out: "Pull me up!"

Great was the amazement of the crowd that had gathered when, on the boy's reaching the top, they found that the rope had been most ingeniously fastened around his waist, under the arms, and so cleverly arranged as also to support the feet. It was manifestly impossible that he could have so arranged the rope. He then proceeded to tell them how the Saint had saved him and how, when the rope was lowered, she fastened it around him. He described her minutely and added that she was very like a little girl, a girl of thirteen, standing in the crowd. The poor lad was drenched from head to foot and besmeared with mud, yet the paper he had snatched from the statue and hidden in his breast was perfectly dry.

A WONDERFUL CURE

Mrs. Raymundo suffered for four years from the worst form of bone disease. She suffered excruciating pains in every part of her body. Her bones became transparent like glass. She could not make the slightest movement, except when a severe spasm of pain shot through her body, and this frequently caused a bone to break. In fact, seven ribs were broken, as well as both arms between the elbow and the wrist. Her collarbone, too, was also badly broken. All her bones were in the state of rapid decay.

She consulted no less than fourteen of the ablest doctors in Portugal, all of whom after using every possible care declared her to be incurable.

At the end of four years she was brought once more to Lisbon to consult a distinguished bone doctor. After seeing the many radiographs [X-rays] and hearing what his fourteen colleagues had said and done, this doctor made a careful examination of the poor patient. He withdrew after his examination and told the husband that all the doctors in the world could do nothing. The disease had already reached an extreme degree and was now attacking the head. She could not possibly live much longer.

Mrs. Raymundo now made a novena to St. Philomena, but at its conclusion felt no better. Notwithstanding this, she commenced a second novena, and on the very first day she received a sign from the Saint, namely, three loud raps on the floor. This filled her with hope and confidence in the Little Saint.

The family asked the Dominican Fathers of Corpo Santo to say a novena of Masses for her intention.

One afternoon her husband came to pray before the statue in the church. He was surprised at seeing a marvelous change of color in the face of the statue and the bright sparkle in the eyes. St. Philomena appeared like a girl in high fever. This was so extraordinary that the poor man sobbed like a child.

On reaching home, he told his daughter what he had seen and declared his conviction that St. Philomena would cure his wife. As Mrs. Raymundo had to go to the hospital in an ambulance for treatment, he asked that one of the Fathers would get into the ambulance at the church door and give the sick lady Holy Communion and then touch her with the relic of St. Philomena. All her hope was in the Little Saint.

This was done, and lo, when the good Father touched the lady with the relic, she was instantly and completely cured! All pains ceased and she was able to move her arms. Strange, she did not realize that she was cured, so that she went on to the hospital, where the doctor saw at a glance the wonderful change in her appearance and exclaimed: "Madam, Madam, what treatment have you been using since I last saw you?"

"I have been using no remedies, Doctor, but I have been praying to St. Philomena." she replied.

"I know nothing of St. Philomena." said the doctor, "but you are as well as I am. Go at once and get a new radiograph."

She did so, and the new radiograph showed a complete and perfect cure.

The surprise in Lisbon was general. The many doctors who had been treating Mrs. Raymundo refused to believe that she was cured. At the invitation of her husband, however, they went to see her. All were dumb-founded at the clear evidence of her cure.

The last doctor she had seen before her cure, the same who declared that all the doctors in the world could not cure her, was a confirmed atheist. On the advice of her confessor, she went to see him. When the servant announced her, he told the man to go back and ask the name again. He could not believe that Mrs. Raymundo was there.

A second time the servant brought the same name, and once more the Doctor sent him back to ask the name. On hearing for the third time the same name, he was still incredulous, and went himself to the waiting room. On seeing the lady, he got a severe shock and became deadly pale; his eyes filled with tears of emotion, and all he could say was: "Madam, Madam, you are indeed cured." He made no attempt to conceal his surprise, but felt her arms and chest and continued to say: "You are cured, you are indeed cured."

When she was leaving, he begged her to call on him again, as he was most interested in the case. She presented him with a copy of the story of St. Philomena, saying: "Doctor, it was she who cured me."

The doctor, who up to then had ridiculed religion, gladly received the little book. He and the other doctors were deeply impressed by the cure.

Chapter 12

WHAT THE THAUMATURGA
DOES FOR SCHOOLS

It is remarkable how quickly devotion to St. Philomena spreads in schools. Boys and girls soon learn to love her, and she quickly becomes their prime favorite. She, on her part, never tires of bestowing on them extraordinary marks of her bounty and friendship. This is more especially the case when they receive her name in Baptism, or take it in Confirmation.

Teachers would do well to place their schools under her protection and erect her statue in a place where the children can easily visit it and adorn it with offerings of flowers, lamps and candles.

Countless times she saved the schools where she is thus honored from the relentless attacks of anticlerical officials, whose sole aim is to destroy religious influence in every shape and form. But her power is manifested in diverse other ways as well. She brings novices to convents in which the numbers are insufficient; teachers to schools where they are required; she finds means of support for those whose financial resources are small and not infrequently fills their schools with pupils. It is no less noticeable that the health of the children rapidly improves wherever the little Wonder-Worker is honored.

This is an account given by a parish priest:

"I was nominated to a large parish which had been splendidly organized by my predecessors. The schools especially were all that one could desire. However, a storm arose, and one of the leading government officials resolved to **stamp religion out** of the minds of the children. The priests, brothers and nuns who were in control of the teaching establishments were for one reason or another ejected, and lay teachers of a bitter anti-clerical type were placed in possession. One of these schools alone had some 500 children, the teachers of which were summarily expelled at the close of the school year. There was no time to find an establishment large enough for such a number, and delay in opening a Catholic school would be fatal.

"We had recourse to St. Philomena, from whom I had already received many proofs of love and affection. By one of these startling coincidences, which those who have experience of the ways of St. Philomena only too well know, we were in three days given possession of a splendid edifice and got a lease of 90 years, though our enemies did all in their power to annul the contract—it was the 10th of August, the Saint's feast [formerly]. We started the necessary works without delay, and so rapidly did these proceed that we were able to open **our own magnificent school** at the beginning of the collegiate year and found we had nearly all of our 500 children safe and sound. We soon built a chapel in our dear saint's honor, in which we placed a beautiful relic. Every year we celebrate her feast with great pomp, while she in turn bestows on us constant and truly marvelous favors."

Here is another incident no less worth-while relating:

"We placed our school under the special protection of St. Philomena and erected her statue not only in our classrooms, but placed one in the dormitory and another in the refectory. Since that time, our children have enjoyed magnificent health; the numbers of pupils have increased considerably and, though we are facing terrific odds, our examinations have been most successful." —S.M.

In the convent school of B., the sisters were in great distress. Their school was far from successful. Sister M. Jane suggested promising Masses and prayers to St. Philomena if they obtained an increase of pupils, and mentioned what appeared to the other members of the community a preposterously large number. The Reverend Mother agreed, however, to the suggestion, but was content to fix a much smaller number than had been proposed, ridiculing as impossible the first proposal. The prayers began, and soon the number indicated by the Reverend Mother was reached, then that proposed by Sister M. Jane, and shortly after, even this was exceeded. Encouraged by what they considered a stupendous favor, the sisters asked for postulants and again had reason to be grateful to the Thaumaturga, who answered their petitions most generously.

In the matter of **examinations**, St. Philomena's influence is especially felt. The successes are notable, the certificates high, and the teachers are frequently amazed at the splendid and at times unanticipated results. A very extraordinary case occurred in Italy.

The staff of teachers in one of the convents became insufficient, and the superioress was at her wit's end to cope with the difficulty. She finally summoned one of the sisters on active duty, and though well aware of her imperfect preparation for the rigorous state examinations, which were conducted by an anticlerical board, she begged the little sister to present herself without delay for the test examination. "O, Mother!" she exclaimed, "you know how unfit I am and how very weak I am in some of the most important subjects." However, seeing the predicament in which her superior found herself, she generously submitted, though with the greatest trepidation.

The examination proved beyond her ability, and some of the questions she made no attempt to answer. Yet she felt that someone was answering for her, and great was her relief when the examiners declared themselves perfectly satisfied and complimented her on her success. She had no doubt that the answers were made by her Little Friend of Mugnano, whom she had confidently invoked.

Though such miraculous interventions as these are not as a rule to be expected, still the Saint's manifest help is ever apparent, and countless students have to thank her for the brilliant success which they have achieved.

Children of Mary, especially, whether attached to public churches or to convent chapels, can do a great deal to propagate devotion to the Little Saint. Pius IX in 1862 declared St. Philomena "**Patroness of the Children of Mary**," and we saw in the vision of Sister Louisa how Our Blessed Mother called her "beloved above all others," a vision which the Curé of Ars had no difficulty in accepting. Therefore, those devoted to Mary may well take St. Philomena as their model and use their influence to make her better known.

Where the devotion has not been introduced, or where a statue is not yet erected, the Children of Mary can easily find means to purchase one and expose it for public veneration. They can very easily make their church or chapel a sanctuary of the Saint. This they may achieve by spreading among the people the story of the wonders which the Saint works and the graces she obtains. In some schools, a supply of cords, medals, and novenas are kept in stock for those who may wish to have them. This decidedly facilitates the propagation of the devotion.

Chapter 13

ANSWERS TO PRAYER

While our great Saint continues to astonish the world with astounding prodigies worked in favor of her clients, on whom she delights to pour down the most abundant blessings, it would be a mistake to imagine that she always bestows her favors by means of extraordinary portents. She no doubt wields a most marvelous power, conferred on her by God, but she is pleased to use it in a great variety of ways.

Sometimes she is most gracious and, if I may use the expression, "human"; whereas, at other times she is even playful. Then again, there are occasions when her answers are given by way of a series of coincidences, perfectly natural in themselves, but so singular and opportune as to point clearly to a guiding hand from above. And lastly, the dear Little Saint will at times show her grave displeasure with those who, after receiving of her bounty, break faith with her and refuse to fulfill what they had solemnly promised. We shall have occasion to see in the following pages the several ways she answers prayer.

HOW ST. PHILOMENA SAVED A CHURCH

Political and anti-clerical feeling ran very high in L. A bomb had been placed in the French church, but fortunately did not do much damage. We were in hourly expectation of a similar outrage in our church. Kind friends, sharing our fears, sent a telegram to the Sanctuary of Mugnano, begging that a novena of Masses should be offered immediately in honor of St. Philomena for the safety of the church, and asking that the last of these should be sung.

On the day that the novena concluded, a large dynamite bomb, surrounded by several dynamite cartridges, was scientifically placed in the church, and the fuse was lighted. Experts declared publicly that it was large enough to blow the whole church to pieces. The bomb was placed in a hidden corner of the building and completely out of sight, so that in the natural order of things there was not the slightest chance of its being seen.

By a series of extraordinary coincidences, the absence of any of which would have proved fatal, the infernal machine was discovered just at the most opportune moment. The way in which the fuse was extinguished was no less strange. The boy who tried to put it out rubbed it in such a way that the military expert, who afterwards examined him, declared that his action was only calculated to further ignite it and cause the explosion to come off more quickly.

The evening previous, a gentleman, whose statement is well worthy of confidence, declared that while praying before the statue of the Saint, he was struck by the flushed appearance of the face and the strange light in the eyes, as if caused by excitement. Fearing that his imagination was playing him a trick, he looked more fixedly at the statue, and his first impressions were more and more confirmed.

We see in this account, first, that a novena of Masses was actually being said for the safety of the church in the Sanctuary of St. Philomena; second, that by a series of extraordinary coincidences the bomb, already ignited, was discovered; third, a trustworthy witness avers that he saw the face of the statue of the Saint as if it were highly excited; fourth, the bomb was discovered on the last day of a novena at Corpo Santo, Lisbon. The third fact is all the more wonderful, as it has been frequently observed in other statues of St. Philomena and may be considered one of the frequent signs given by the Saint.

Is it too much to believe that we owe our safety to the protection of the Virgin Martyr?

REMARKABLE CURES

Two ladies came to me one day and told me that a little friend of theirs was very ill and asked if I would lend them my relic of St. Philomena. It was not convenient for me to give it at the moment. They called again and told me that **the child was actually dying** and again begged me to lend them the relic. I gave it to them at once.

On arriving at the child's home, they found the little one at the point of death. The mother was frantic with grief and implored the two doctors present to say that there was some hope. They told her frankly that there was none and warned her that the end was very near.

The two ladies arrived at this moment with the relic and placed it near the little sufferer, whose face already wore the hue of death. In a few minutes the worn-out frame showed signs of returning energy, the eyes opened, the breathing became natural and the little one began to play with a pet bird. St. Philomena once more had triumphed over death.

One of those who witnessed the scene begged that the relic might be given to her to take to a friend who likewise lay dying. She was suffering from **a fatal tumor**, and her doctor had told her plainly to make her last preparations, for any moment might be her last. All he could now do for her was to give some soothing remedies to relieve the pains. The poor patient presented a sad sight, swollen as she was to a huge size.

Her friend brought the relic from the home of the little child and placed it near the sick lady, and, lo, the wondrous power of the Thaumaturga was again put forth so that the sick woman was enabled in a short time to make a long journey to her distant home!

I had a grave attack of **pleurisy** accompanied with excruciating pains, high fever and an irregular pulse. Two and a half pints of liquid had gathered in the pleura, and the case was considered very grave. I had on the cord of the dear Little Saint and felt great confidence in her help.

At the most acute stage of the sickness, two friends heard of my danger and at once made a promise to have a novena of Masses said at the Sanctuary of the Saint in Mugnano. They asked the Little Thaumaturga not to wait for the Masses, but to show her power at once. The answer to their prayers was instantaneous. When the doctor, who had left me in great anxiety the previous day, returned and took my pulse, he was manifestly amazed.

"Why," he exclaimed, "your pulse today is like a good English watch! Let us see your temperature." On his examining the thermometer, a new cry of surprise burst from his lips: "My dear Sir, you have not even fever today!" He then proceeded to sound me and found further cause for wonder. The liquid had disappeared from the pleura.

Later on he said to me: "Your recovery is clearly miraculous, and it seems to me a very striking answer to prayer."

Sister Malachy, Mercy Convent, L., writes:
"I had a grievous attack of **erysipelas**, aggravated by other grave complications. My state was desperate, and I received the Last Sacraments. St. Philomena was invoked in my favor, and I was blessed with her relic. Immediately, the fever—which was at 104°—fell, so that my temperature in a few hours became normal, and I was pronounced to be out of danger. I attribute it all to St. Philomena."

Mademoiselle Helene was suffering for two years from an **interior growth**, the nature of which the doctors could not ascertain. Finally, the growth reached such a size that the physicians decided to perform an operation, not without fear of the gravest results. The operating surgeon gave the nurses instructions to be prepared for the worst.

During her illness, the good lady had sent up many and fervent prayers to St. Philomena, to whom she was sincerely devoted. Many Masses were said too for her recovery, some of which were offered in the Sanctuary of Mugnano. The good custodians of the Sanctuary joined their hearty supplications with the prayers offered by the priest at the altar.

Mlle Helene's confessor, fully alive to the gravity of the case, gave her a last absolution immediately before the operation took place. He then went to the chapel of the hospital and made the following prayer to St. Philomena: "Dear Saint, if you had wished, you could have prevented the necessity of an operation. Now at least show us by some clear sign that you are with the dear patient. I should like, for instance, that at the conclusion of the operation the doctors should say to me: 'It was a splendid operation,' or, 'Everything went on magnificently.' Make it *manifest*, dear Saint, that you are with us."

The operation proved to be a very serious one. Doctors and nurses were all surprised at the enormous size of the growth. It succeeded, however, beyond their highest hopes. The patient, strange to say, felt no consequent pains, except the inconvenience caused by the chloroform. The convalescence was rapid and the cure perfect. Immediately after the operation, the confessor went to speak to the doctors, one of whom said at once: "My dear sir, the operation was *splendid*." Chatting with the second doctor, he in turn said, "Why, everything passed off *magnificently*." These were the very words stipulated by the priest in his prayer to St. Philomena.

The nurses, learning of this prayer and seeing the marvelous results of the operation, resolved to test the power of the Saint in another very difficult case.

A French journalist had been brought to the hospital suffering from **a malignant tumor**. His soul was suffering quite as much as his body, for though nominally a Catholic—he had been baptized—he never received the other Sacraments nor heard Mass. He was not married to the woman he called his wife. Worst of all, the good Sisters were strictly forbidden, by the rules of the hospital, to speak of religion unless the patient expressly desired it.

A novena to St. Philomena began. The unfortunate man of his own free will wished to know something about religion. After some days, he went to Confession, communicated and was married.

The doctors attempted an operation but, on seeing the awful state of the tumor, immediately desisted. They saw no possible hope for him.

The novena continued. Days passed, and the patient began to show signs of improvement. The doctors once more attempted an operation and this time with the best results.

The patient in due course left the hospital cured in soul and body.

Mademoiselle Marie Guido was suffering from **acute headaches**, which developed symptoms of the gravest kind.

She went, accompanied by her sister, to consult the ablest physician in the city. During the consultation, she suddenly fell at the doctor's feet as if dead.

He summoned one of his colleagues, and both made a minute examination of the patient. At its conclusion, he turned to her sister and said: "I have no hopes. She has lost her mind and I fear her life. I can't give the slightest hope of her ultimate recovery. The mind is irrevocably lost, and as far as I can see, there is no chance even that she can live."

She was taken to her home, hovering between life and death. A friend who knew of her great devotion to St. Philomena made a promise to the Saint in her name. The morning found her improved. As her further progress was doubtful, the same kind friend made a further promise to have a novena of Masses said in Mugnano and offered a very generous alms.

The results were wonderful, and when the doctors called to see her, they were astounded. She regained perfect health and soon became as well as ever.

My brother-in-law suffered for many years from **a weak chest**. During this period, he had severe attacks. At the time of which I write, his life was despaired of, so much so that the distinguished physician who attended him warned his wife that there was no hope and that she had better summon those of his friends who wished to see him before death.

When the sad news reached me—I was living at a long distance away—I wrote at once and suggested having recourse to St. Philomena. A large picture of the Saint was placed in the poor patient's room and a lamp burned before it.

The arrival of the Saint's picture in the house was the signal for the most abundant graces. Not only did she obtain the dying man's cure, but from that day forward spiritual and temporal blessings have been showered on the family.

His Lordship the saintly Bishop of Meliapor says:
"I have indeed learned to love St. Philomena and am most grateful to her. She has given me many signs of her powerful intercession. On one occasion, I was

in need of funds for my Missionary College, and she
obtained for me no less a sum than 20,000 escudos.
On another occasion, we had to begin important
improvements in the College of Cucujães, and these
unfortunately threatened to be the cause of serious
inconvenience. I promised St. Philomena that if she
helped me and had the improvements concluded at
a certain date, I would reopen an oratory which had
been closed and dedicate it in her honor. She did
all I asked her, and I on my part opened the oratory
and dedicated it to her. Now I beg you to help me to
procure a large and beautiful statue of the dear Little
Saint. I wish it to be about six feet high."

Here is how the Bishop of Algarve came to know
St. Philomena:

I published a small work on St. Philomena and sent
it to the Bishop of Algarve (now Bishop of Oporto),
requesting him to write a few lines of approbation.

The evening before he received my letter and the
book, he was with an old friend, who said to him: "I do
not know, my Lord, what you'll think of me, but I confess that I have no devotion to the Saints. The Sacred
Heart and the Blessed Mother of God are my friends";
but he added, sotto voce, "there is always one little
exception." The Bishop overheard these last words
and said: "If I may enquire, who is the little exception?" "St. Philomena, my Lord, and I don't know why.
One thing is certain: I never go to bed at night without
praying to her."

The book and my letter arrived next morning, and it
was with the greatest avidity that His Lordship read the
book, for he wanted to know who this St. Philomena

was, of whom his old friend had spoken the evening before. He perused the work with intense delight and wrote to me to say that he was coming to stay with us for some days and would willingly give me the approbation I wished for.

In the course of his visit, I met him one evening on the stairs. "Do you know where I have been?" he asked me.

"No, my Lord," I replied.

"Well, I have just been to the church to pay a visit to your St. Philomena. I made a bargain with her to the effect that, if she obtained for me all I asked, I would put her statue in my cathedral and have a special solemn feast celebrated in her honor. Come to my room and I will write the letter of approbation you asked for with all my heart."

Some weeks elapsed and the good Bishop came again to honor our house with his presence. After supper when we were chatting with him, he suddenly turned to me and exclaimed, "She has it!" I did not perceive what he meant, so he said again, "I tell you, she has it!"

"I beg your pardon, my Lord," I replied, "I do not understand. Who is 'she' and what has she got?" "St. Philomena, of course," he answered. "She has got her statue in my cathedral. She did all I asked of her and, by the way, did not allow me to buy the statue, for a good lady of the town had the happy inspiration to offer me one."

I may add that His Lordship is a man of great height and grand physique, big in every way. His ideas and his demands are, I believe, in keeping with his physical build, so that if St. Philomena gave him *all* he asked, it is fair to infer that she well deserves a statue in his cathedral.

A young lady called on me some time ago. She was in great grief. She had been engaged to be married and had been intensely happy. Quite unexpectedly and without the slightest fault on her part, all her hopes were shattered **and the marriage broken off**. I did all I could to comfort her, and though her grief was poignant, I could not help admiring her magnificent resignation to God's will.

"Go," I said, "to the statue of St. Philomena in the church, and beg her, if it be God's will, to settle this awful difficulty." "What prayer ought I say to her?" she enquired. "Promise," I counselled her, "to make a novena of Communions, and commence at once." Four days later, I was again called down to see a lady. It was my former visitor, radiant with joy. "Father," she said, "it is all right. I began my novena of Communions to St. Philomena, and all difficulties have been overcome, and we shall soon be married."

One afternoon, the Countess of G. was announced. It did not take me long to see that she was in sore trouble. As I was intimately connected with the family, I enquired: "Countess, you are evidently in trouble. Can I help you?"

"Yes," she answered, "I have to face **a very cruel ordeal** tonight. It is dreadful." She related the circumstances. I suggested some possible ways of escape. "No, no," she replied, "it is absolutely impossible to get out of it. I have only to face the trouble, but I do dread it."

"Well," I said, "seeing that there is no human hope, why not try St. Philomena?" "It is quite useless. I never remember that a prayer of mine was heard," she replied.

"Try at all events, Countess; promise the Saint a novena of Communions, and we shall see if she will help you."

"I promise," she answered, "but I don't expect anything."

Next morning, her ladyship was again announced, and at an unusually early hour.

"Ah," she said, "this was in truth an answer direct from Heaven! Scarcely had I arrived home after my interview with you last evening than one difficulty after another was removed without the smallest effort on my part, and so I was delivered from that hateful situation."

A poor lady of the city of Braga, in the north of Portugal, wrote to me begging for prayers and asking if I could send her a relic or an image of St. Philomena. She had **suffered much** on the occasion of the birth of her children, all of whom were either born dead or died immediately after birth. She was soon again to give birth to another child and was with good reason in great consternation. She had just read a little work published by me on St. Philomena and was inspired to put all her confidence in the holy Virgin Martyr.

The child was born some time after our interchange of correspondence, and the poor lady asked the nurse how it fared. She answered roughly, "Just like all the rest—dead, or as good as dead! There is no hope whatever for it." The poor mother then besought a second attendant to touch the baby with the image of the Saint. Immediately, the infant moaned and began to give signs of increasing vitality. In a short time the little one developed into a beautiful baby.

PROMISES NOT FULFILLED

Father Sebastian Bowden of the Oratory, in the little work he edited on St. Philomena, relates the following incidents, which are well worth our serious attention.

A married woman who had suffered for twelve years from **an incurable malady**, which had cost her such large sums that she was reduced to poverty, said one day before a miraculous picture of the Saint: "My Saint, if thou art so powerful before God, let this evil pass from me, and I promise thee 'such and such a gold ornament,'" naming one that was worth more than ten ducats. No sooner had she made this promise than she was entirely healed, and she herself promulgated this favor.

But for three months, she refused to fulfill her promise. Her husband endeavored to persuade her to do so for conscience sake, and at length she offered, not the ornament she had promised, but another worth only two ducats. In that moment her disease broke out with greater violence than before, and not all the prayers that were offered for her could again obtain her cure.

There lived at Montemarano a husband and wife **who had no children**. They had recourse to St. Philomena, and they vowed that if they were blessed with a daughter they would call her Philomena and carry her to Mugnano to thank the Saint. Their request was granted, and they fulfilled the first part of the vow, but not the second. The husband wished to accomplish it, but the wife turned a deaf ear to his entreaties.

The little Philomena was more than two years old, beautiful and clever. Hearing that a feast was to be celebrated in Castelvetere, a neighboring village, in honor of St. Philomena, the wife said she would take the child there to fulfill the vow, instead of to Mugnano. The husband protested, but she insisted and went to spend the feast at Castelvetere. That same night at bedtime, the little Philomena ran up to her parents, contrary to custom, and kissed them both; then, calling them Papa and Mama, she suddenly expired. In their terrible consternation, the parents hastened to Mugnano to appease the just anger of the holy Martyr, lest worse should befall;[1] and there they related that they had previously had several terrible warnings and punishments from which they had been delivered by renewing their vow, and yet they had never fulfilled it till then.

_____

1   Though the author speaks of St. Philomena chastising people for failure to fulfill vows and promises, it is actually God who, in His divine justice, metes out punishments, measuring the chastisement to fit the guilt. "Vengeance belongeth to me." (Heb. 10:30). Our Lady and the Saints are models of compassion and succor, never of vengeance or justice. Should we fail to fulfill our part of vows or promises for favors received, it is God who rightly sends punishments for this. The fact that He would do so in such a marked degree for failure to fulfill promises made to St. Philomena serves to emphasize the great intercessory power this Saint possesses in granting favors. As God is so gracious in bestowing favors through her, it would seem that, conversely, He is equally stern with the recalcitrant recipients of those favors who fail to fulfill their promises. —*Editor*, 1993.

St. Philomena is so desirous to show us favors that she not only rewards those who propagate devotion to her, but even chastises those who refuse to make her known.

An Archdeacon of Ascoli, in Italy, received a relic of the Saint from a lady who begged him to spread the devotion to her. But believing that there was more of natural zeal than of true devotion in the request, he shut up the relic and even refused it to the Bishop, who wished to use it for a solemn feast in honor of the Saint. This refusal was much talked of, and he was warned that some punishment would befall him. He replied that he had no fear of the Saints—who wish us well—and that if it was the will of God, some sign would be vouchsafed him.

St. Philomena took him at his word, and on the third of May, 1832, at noonday, the light seemed to fade from his eyes, the objects in the room gradually disappeared, and he became totally blind. This was no attack of giddiness; there was no natural cause for it—it was something more; it was supernatural. His thoughts turned at once to St. Philomena, the refusal of her relic and the threatened chastisement. His hand sought the reliquary and he prayed fervently to the Saint. But his blindness lasted. Overwhelmed by the thought that it might be forever, he rose to seek consolation elsewhere.

But he said to himself: "If it be the will of God, should I not be content? But how can there be contentment or joy for a creature plunged in darkness, for whom the light of Heaven shines in vain?" Unable to calm his agitation, he returned in half an hour to his oratory and began to pray to the Saint with full confidence of being heard. Then, as he took the relic to bless himself, the darkness instantly vanished. He read the inscription on the reliquary: *Ex ossibus et indusio S. Filumenae, V. et M.* ["from the bones and garment of St. Philomena, Virgin and Martyr"], and his sight returned completely.

In the fullness of his heart he poured forth his thanksgivings to St. Philomena, then hastened to his bishop. The Bishop carefully took down his deposition of the miracle, and the Archdeacon became the introducer and fervent promoter of the devotion to the holy Martyr in Ascoli, where she worked many striking miracles.

DERISION PUNISHED

Very severe punishments fall upon those who deride her miracles and who, led astray by the desolating philosophy of the present day, pride themselves upon being unprejudiced and hold that to believe things contrary to the ordinary laws of nature is fit only for the credulous and those of weak minds. Many of these have been struck down by unknown and incurable diseases. Numbers have died at the very moment they were deriding the wonders worked by God through this Saint. Many families of high station, full of this pride, were reduced to poverty, and on the contrary, in consequence of these events, some of the most devoted to the Saint are those who were formerly among the indevout.

In a great city the first feast of St. Philomena was being celebrated with much splendor. A certain ecclesiastic, seeing the rejoicing and fervor, said contemptuously,

"Did we want another Saint here? Have we not feasts enough?" And murmuring thus, he went home. The bystanders were much shocked and began whispering among themselves that the Saint would not leave him unpunished. The words were scarcely out of their mouths when they beheld his servants running in search of doctors, for he had been struck down by a mortal illness and lay as if dead upon the ground. He shortly after expired.

For several years, two rich men in Naples had carried on a lawsuit against a village of poor peasants; the latter implored the aid of St. Philomena, their patron. Justice was already inclining to their side, on which lay the right. But by cunning craft and by interest, the brothers gained their cause—to the ruin and desolation of the poor villagers. Again they had recourse to St. Philomena, but the haughty brothers derided them, saying, "Now we shall see what St. Philomena will do for you. We are coming to the country and then you will see if St. Philomena can deliver you." To these impious words a poor woman employed in their house replied: "Gentlemen, do not outrage the Saint. She is not like one of us; you cannot mock her with impunity."

"What will she do to us?" said they, jeeringly, and the poor woman replied, "She can deprive you of life before you set foot in our village."

To this their only answer was scorn, and they set forth. As they drew near the last village before arriving at their journey's end, their carriage leaned to one side and nearly fell down a precipice, but just escaped being overturned. This so affected one of the brothers that he was forced to stop in that village to rest, and in less than an hour he was a corpse. This made a terrible impression upon his brother, and he also, although up to that moment in perfect health, fell down dead before the body of his brother had grown cold.

This event spread in all those parts the glory of St. Philomena and the power of her protection; and those poor villagers who had been saved by her repaired to her shrine to pray, in the goodness of their hearts, for the repose of the souls of their oppressors.

And now that this labor of love is finished, we hasten to offer it to our dear Saint as a token, insignificant indeed, but not for that the less sincere, of our deep gratitude, love and affection. May she bless this little work and make it fruitful of good, so that its readers may learn to know and love her and so taste of the richness of her bounty.

With our humble offering, we—the Priest and the Soldier—place ourselves, our dear ones, our hopes, our fears and our labors at the feet of the dear Thaumaturga.

Supplement I

ST. PHILOMENA VINDICATED

Since the publication of *St. Philomena—The Wonder-Worker* in February, 1927, we have received very many kind and encouraging letters from bishops, priests and lay folk, as well as from colleges and convents, where the little work has found great favor. From these we select a few for publication; we trust they will rejoice the clients of St. Philomena and lead others to love and trust the "dear Little Saint." Some of our correspondents, while wishing to make known the graces they received, prefer that their names should remain unknown, a condition that we all the more readily accept as it will, we hope, induce others to send us their own experiences, confident of receiving similar treatment, if they so wish.

Friends, too, have put questions regarding the Saint, calling our attention to various items of criticism which caught their eye in some newspaper or review. An answer to most of these queries will be found by a careful perusal of the pages of *St. Philomena—The Wonder-Worker.*

This little book was written rather as a work of popular devotion, with the aim of making St. Philomena better known and loved, than with the idea of answering controversialists or pretending to deep historical research. Still, it contains more than sufficient information to satisfy the sincere searcher after truth and to allay the doubts of any troubled client of Saint Philomena.

We take the opportunity, however, of directing attention to the fact that the doubts and difficulties raised are not new. They have all been subjected in Rome to thorough examination; and the investigations made, so far from lessening the cult of the Saint, have only served to increase and intensify it.

As we already stated, **the Roman Pontiffs**, one after another, from the date of the discovery of the relics until now, approved, confirmed and recommended the devotion to **St. Philomena**, **Virgin** and **Martyr** and **Wonder-Worker**.

Constant and wonderful miracles, answers to prayer, abundant graces and blessings have been and still continue to be the result of the devotion all the world over. Thus the Almighty Himself would seem to ratify the decisions of His Vicars on earth.

His Holiness, Pope Pius XI, also declared that when the Pope makes a declaration, Catholics must feel that he is speaking after mature and thorough consideration. And certainly in the case of St. Philomena, there was long, thorough and most profound study and scrutiny of facts before Rome spoke.

FACTS AND EVIDENCE

The accumulated evidence of facts, scientific investigations, the opinions of specialists, the constant miracles, the extraordinary spread of the devotion and its beneficent results, the decisions of Roman Congregations and the Supreme authority and example of the Sovereign Pontiffs themselves seem to be made light of because some accidental details are not forthcoming, or because the opinion of one or another scientist does not tally with the general belief of the faithful.

That discussions arose regarding the exact date of the Saint's life and death, of the manner of her martyrdom, and regarding the slabs which enclosed her precious remains, can be no matter of surprise if we remember that she lived close to 2,000 years ago. Similar—not to say very much graver—doubts have been entertained regarding relatively recent events, yet no one calls into question the events themselves.

Archaeologists, historians, philosophers, savants in every branch of science are far from being unanimous in their conclusions, much less are their assertions infallible. That one or another of these savants should differ from his colleagues on one or another detail, or that he should fail to accept the testimony of other very weighty authorities, does not in any way militate against facts which have behind them strong and reliable evidence.

Truth welcomes discussion, and controversy only tends to further our comprehension of facts, provided, however, that the discussion and controversy *are just and fair.*

It is not, however, either honest or fair to state the arguments for one side and ignore the evidence for the other, to repeat doubts and raise difficulties that were raised and answered many times before without informing the reader that such has been the case, nor is it just to quote one authority against a thesis and make no mention of a host of others in its favor. Still less should one expect to see a doubt concerning an accidental detail used to militate against a devotion which has such a body of evidence and such weighty authority in its favor as the cult of St. Philomena.

THE BLOOD OF ST. PHILOMENA

One of our good friends called our attention to the fact that a distinguished scholar had stated that the finding of vials of a matter which purported to be blood did not prove that the remains found in the corresponding loculus (tomb) were those of a martyr, whence it was left to be inferred that St. Philomena was not necessarily a martyr!

The statement, as it stands, is very misleading. A full explanation of the facts will throw not a little light on the subject.

Sometimes, it is true, substances were placed near the tombs for the purpose of dissipating the foul odors which were naturally not uncommon in the badly ventilated underground vaults of the Catacombs. That of course is not blood. Does it follow, though, that the substance contained in *other* vials, which has been declared, on the best authority to be blood, and has been found not only on the outside but on the inside of the loculi, is not blood? Certainly not. Let us remember, for we have it on the most irrefragable authority, that one of the well-known devotions of the early Christians was to gather the blood of the martyrs and preserve it as their greatest treasure. This they did at considerable risk to themselves. Now the Catacombs were huge reliquaries, and nowhere could this most cherished treasure be preserved so securely and so fittingly.

Next, the contents of these vials have been frequently analyzed according to the most up-to-date methods, by Catholic and non-Catholic scientists alike, who have declared themselves fully satisfied that the substance in question is blood.

The blood of St. Philomena has been the instrument of the most wonderful prodigies, witnessed by countless persons of unimpeachable authority. These prodigies have been fully dealt with in Chapter 5 of the work. We content ourselves here with quoting the words of two learned Cardinals.

Cardinal Ruffo Scilla, who affixed the seals to the reliquary containing the blood of St. Philomena, declares in his solemn deposition: "And we ourselves have seen her blood changed into several brilliant precious stones, into gold and silver likewise."

Cardinal Dechamps, Archbishop of Malines, made a pilgrimage to Mugnano and thus describes what he saw:

". . . I saw above all, that precious blood shed for the love of virginity. It was at first dull and hardened, and behold! Jesus Christ, by communicating to it a ray of the glory of the soul which offered it to Him, renders it dazzling as the rainbow. It is truly marvelous. I had read accounts of it, but now I can say that I have seen it with my own eyes."

These explanations convey a very different idea from the bald statement above.

MISLEADING STATEMENTS

We venture to express the opinion that the publication by some popular newspaper or magazine of one-sided and therefore misleading statements can only lessen the simple faith of the ordinary Catholic and do incalculable mischief to souls. If published, such views should be reserved for more scientific reviews, where scholar meets scholar and where the discussion of a doubt is not likely to be construed into an argument against the main body of evidence. At all events, the case must be stated fully and fairly, and then the cause of the Saint will have all to gain and nothing to lose.

Regarding letters recently published by a well-known Catholic newspaper, a copy of which was sent to us, we confess that we were amazed at the temerity of those who were responsible for their publication.

Not so very long ago eminent scholars and distinguished ecclesiastics were most severely censured by Rome for faults of irreverence and disrespect far less grave than those committed by the above-mentioned writers. The traducers of devotion towards St. Philomena have dared to declare that St. Philomena was a pretended saint, that she was neither a Saint nor a Virgin nor a Martyr! These contentions were based chiefly on the authority of Père Delahaye, S.J., while the name of Professor Marucchi was also dragged into the controversy.

In reply, we first of all call attention to the fact that these declarations are flagrantly in opposition to the decisions of the Roman congregations and constitute a most disrespectful and rash denial of the solemn decrees and repeated declarations of the Roman Pontiffs themselves. That in itself is answer sufficient to the critics of St. Philomena. They are acting in defiance of Rome.

But for the honor of our dear Saint and with her help, we will go further into the matter and allow an eminent Jesuit to answer in detail the rash statements.

CORRECTING A GRAVE MISAPPREHENSION

As far back as 1906, the distinguished Father Buonavenia, a Jesuit archaeologist of the Pontifical Gregorian University, which is so justly esteemed in the whole Catholic world as a center of learning, published a work of 200 pages entitled *Controversia sul celeberrimo epitaffio di St. Philomena V.M.* We possess a copy presented to us by the author.

This erudite work was the result of long and most careful research. The distinguished writer had every facility for getting first class information, and of these opportunities he availed himself to the full. He went in person and saw everything that was to be seen regarding the question at issue; he consulted the ablest men of science; he questioned most carefully those who could shed any light on the finding of the relics; in a word, he left no stone unturned to get the fullest and most accurate information. He examined the question as an archaeologist, as an historian and as a theologian.

In the first place, he proves in this able work that Professor Marucchi was under a grave misapprehension regarding the vial of blood found in the tomb of St. Philomena, and he shows that the vial was not found on the outside of the tomb, as the professor erroneously affirmed, but *inside* and near the head of the Saint!

This correction of the false impression on the part of Professor Marucchi, though apparently trivial, has a very important bearing on the question in dispute, as Father Buonavenia distinctly points out. Always the scholar and the gentleman, the good Father does not make light of Professor Marucchi's ability as a scientist, for he is careful to show that the error was not so much a false archaeological deduction as an historical mistake. He proves that the authority on which Professor Marucchi bases his statement, viz., Santiucci Sebastiano, is worthless and that *all the other writers* held the contrary view, namely, that the vial was found inside the loculus.

Secondly, he shows that Professor Marucchi, while under a misapprehension (caused by erroneous information and not the result of an archaeological deduction), did not share the extravagant ideas of Père Delahaye, but was very respectful to the Holy See.

Thirdly, Father Buonavenia laments bitterly that he is obliged to take up his pen and write against a brother Jesuit, whom he shows to be acting in flagrant contradiction to the declarations and solemn decrees of several Popes, most notably Gregory XVI, whose decree relating to the Saint he shows to have the full weight of a solemn decree!

Then he asks what Fr. Delahaye, S.J. holds. He answers that unfortunately Father Delahaye declares that he holds the same opinion as Lenorment, which is that St. Philomena is "in pretense a Saint, but in reality she is neither a Saint, nor a Virgin, nor a Martyr, nor a Philomena."

And this when Popes declare solemnly, repeatedly and after most mature investigations that *Saint Philomena is a Saint,* a Virgin and a Martyr, and a Wonder-Worker!

Finally, he quotes decisions and acts of Pope Pius X in which that Pope, then reigning, commanded that the decisions and declarations made by his predecessors regarding St. Philomena were to be in nowise altered!

How is it that the publishers above mentioned never allude in any way to Father Buonavenia's work, though he was clearly the person who wrote most extensively on the question and in answer to both Père Delahaye and Marucchi?

It is incomprehensible that any Catholic dare contradict so flagrantly the Holy Father himself and repudiate contemptuously the decisions of the Roman Congregations. How can Bishops expect respect, obedience and submission if it be denied to Christ's Vicar? Nor can attenuating circumstances be pleaded. It cannot be urged that the decisions and decrees in question were made in far-off centuries when Roman procedure was less rigorous, nor can any doubt be raised as to the authenticity of the documents or the accuracy of their interpretation. The decisions are modern and made with the utmost caution, for which Rome is so justly famous, so as to ensure unerring accuracy. These are the decisions that some Catholics dare to impugn and deny.

It must strike any thoughtful Catholic as strange that one of the most loved and lovable of Saints, whose cult is producing such marvelous results for good all over the world and is being blessed every day by constant, striking and well-authenticated wonders, is so frequently singled out as **an object of attack**, not by Protestants or Free-thinkers, but **by Catholics themselves**. It reminds one of the spleen and envy with which the Scribes and

Pharisees sought to disparage the holiness and belittle the miracles of our Divine Master, who they alleged was in collusion with Beelzebub, the Prince of Devils!

The disciple is not above his Master, nor is the servant above his Lord, so that clients of St. Philomena must not be alarmed if a like treatment is meted out to their saintly Protectress.

Well might she ask her traducers, as did the Divine Master before her: "For which of my good works do you stone me?" Wherever her devotion is established, the sick are healed, the sorrowful are consoled, sinners are converted and God showers down His grace and works His prodigies to show how pleased He is at the honor paid to His servant. For which of these good works is devotion to her decried?

"Oh!" exclaim her enemies, like the enemies of our Divine Lord, "it is not her works we cry out against, but because devotion to her is mere ignorant credulity on the part of the faithful, who are duped into honoring her."

So then the Sovereign Pontiffs, **Popes Gregory XVI, Leo XII, Pius IX, Leo XIII, Pius X** and **Benedict XV,** the many Cardinals, Bishops, and savants who are among her clients, the multitudes of enlightened Catholics all the world over are all forsooth "dupes" of their imagination, ignorant and over-credulous!

To sum up, the Roman Congregations and the Popes themselves, using their supreme authority, have declared emphatically and repeatedly that **St. Philomena** is a **Saint**, a **Virgin**, a **Martyr** and a **Wonder-Worker**.

Those who dare deny that such is the case are acting thereby in open defiance of the authority of Rome.

If, notwithstanding all this, there continue to be

carping critics and others who allow themselves to be led astray by their utterances, we can only bewail the fact and feel sorry that they refuse to get a share in the great graces so generously bestowed by this Thaumaturga.

We, on the other hand, declare ourselves super-abundantly satisfied, and so with God's help we shall remain until our dying day, fervent and loving clients of the "Dear Little Saint."

E.D.M.[1]

---

1 Fr. O'Sullivan referred to himself by the initials E.D.M., which stand for *Enfant de Marie*—"Child of Mary."—*Editor*, 1993.

Supplement 2

LETTERS FROM READERS

From a Seminarian

My dear Rev. Father:

I should be grateful if you published the following striking favors granted me by St. Philomena. I read *St. Philomena—The Wonder-Worker* and, conceiving a great confidence in the Saint, began a novena for several important intentions.

As you may be aware, a report of each student is sent frequently by the authorities of the College to his Bishop, and the Bishop as a rule either personally or through his secretary signifies his pleasure or displeasure at the conduct and progress of the student. I am one of the oldest students in the College and had not received for a considerable time any notification of the sentiments of my Bishop towards me. Naturally, I was in great sorrow, fearing that his Lordship was not satisfied with me, and consequently doubts regarding my vocation began to trouble me seriously.

Secondly, I had, owing to ill health, contracted what was for me a heavy debt, which I was utterly unable to pay off.

Thirdly, I was in much need of special books for my studies, but had no money to get them.

Lastly, I was desirous of procuring something for my room, but again I was confronted with the same difficulty—no money and no hopes of any.

On the last two days of the novena, I received a striking answer to my prayer. Most unexpectedly, a friend gave me what I so much needed for my room. Next, I was not only put in the way of paying off my debts, but even of putting something aside for future needs. This, too, was altogether unlooked for.

Thirdly, I received a letter with money for the books I required, with a promise of further donations.

Lastly, I received a letter so amiable and encouraging from my Bishop as filled me with the greatest joy.

All those favors on the last two days of my novena.

Let me add that I had not breathed a word of my needs to anyone, except to St. Philomena.

The students to whom I have since spoken of these facts are very deeply impressed and I trust that a great devotion to the Wonder-Worker will be the result of all this.

I remain, dear Rev. Father,

Yours sincerely,

J. J.

From a Happy Couple

London

Mr. and Mrs. Staplemax had been married four years. Our Lord, in the ways of His Providence, had not blessed their union with children. While resigned to His holy will, they were still eagerly desirous of having at least an heir to their name and property. Their hope, as the years passed, grew gradually lesser.

Hearing of the wonderful power of St. Philomena, of her love for and kindness to her clients, they resolved to place all their confidence in her intercession. They began to invoke her aid and made the promises their devotion suggested.

Little did they guess what wonders the dear Little Saint was to work in their behalf!

In the month of January following, what was not their delight when St. Philomena sent them two beautiful children! In December of the same year, twins were again born to them, so that in twelve months they were the happy parents of four darling children, one for each year of their married lives!

Lisbon, December 11, 1925

Dear Father:

I have received recently two great blessings from St. Philomena. My wife suffers dreadfully on the occasion of the birth of our children, though she has the assistance of the most competent nurses.

On the last occasion, she suffered even more than usual, but we placed the medal of St. Philomena on her neck, and, thank God, our baby was born under the happiest circumstances possible, and without any medical assistance, for doctor and nurse failed us at the last moment. It seemed as though St. Philomena herself came to our rescue.

Five days later the child fell so grievously ill that

both our doctors feared the case was hopeless. Again we appealed to St. Philomena, who restored the baby to splendid health.

I feel that you will be pleased to hear this good news, and I too should be grateful if you published the facts in thanksgiving to the dear Wonder-Worker.

Yours sincerely,
T. Mattos

Liverpool, January 1926

My dear Helen,

I read the nice little book you sent me, *St. Philomena— The Wonder-Worker,* and began at once to pray to the dear Saint. At first she did not seem to listen to my prayers.

I spoke of the book to our Rector, who was seemingly not much impressed with what I said. He appeared to be rather sceptical regarding Saint Philomena. When next I saw him, he was suffering from a sharp attack of influenza, with the usual disagreeable symptoms. I sent him the book, which he commenced to read. The story of the Saint's marvelous power impressed him strongly, and laying down the book, he said: "St. Philomena, cure me, and I will spread your devotion." He was at once cured and is now keeping his promise; he has passed on the book to a sick parishioner and has said Mass in honor of the Wonder-Worker.

Another Letter from the
Same Client of the Saint

Since my last letter, I am glad to say that our dear Saint has done wonders for me. May she be forever blessed. My sister, Mrs. Rosewat, has wonderful faith in and love for her. She has sold hundreds of copies of the little book. What favors will she not receive?

Michelstown, Ireland
December 19, 1925

I am justly proud of calling myself a friend of St. Philomena, for she is in truth most loving, human and generous. My one regret is not to have known her before. How much might I have obtained from her intercession! I can never do enough for her, and if only I could inspire others with the like faith in and love for her which I have myself, it would indeed be glorious. She is ever giving me something new; I turn to her in all my troubles, and she never fails me.

"Blessed be God in His Saints!"

From a Dominican Nun

St. Philomena's life is really lovely and kindles in the heart of any one who reads it devotion to the dear Little Saint. All who have read it in our community are praying to the Thaumaturga.

—S. M. T.

Lisbon, June 30, 1926

Dear Rev. Father:

You will be pleased to hear that I went to visit St. Philomena's shrine at Mugnano. My husband and I were most anxious that God should give us a little heir, but there seemed no possible hope of such a happy event. Finally, I put the matter into St. Philomena's hands, promising her to take the child, if she obtained it for me, and have it baptized in her own Sanctuary.

Thanks to her powerful intercession, I am now the happy mother of two children. Oh! I am so grateful to our dear Saint! I go almost every Sunday to the Church of Corpo Santo, which is very far away from my home, simply because I wish to visit and pray to the dear Little Saint, who is so much loved and venerated in that church.

(Signed)

The faith of this lady, whom we know personally, is indeed very great, for though her means are moderate she joyfully undertook the long and expensive journey from her home to Naples in fulfillment of her promise.

The Following We Received
from Mrs. Colonel G.

London

My excuse for troubling you with this letter is that I am a most grateful client of St. Philomena. I read the delightful book, *St. Philomena—The Wonder-Worker,* and it brought me great comfort and help. The Saint has done wonders for me. Let me just mention three facts. Some time ago, I was suffering from a bad nervous breakdown, and though I consulted several eminent physicians, I got no relief. I read of St. Philomena's "pill." This, as you know, is the popular title for the tiny prayer printed on fine paper and swallowed or mixed with one's food. I believe they come from the Sanctuary. At the same time, I commenced a novena for the Saint's feast of August 11. From the very beginning, I felt an improvement, which gradually increased and ended in my complete recovery; this was the cause of great astonishment to my friends.

The Almighty was pleased to send me still another cross in the shape of a very grave and painful illness, as a result of which I suffered from such weakness in my legs that, without any previous warning, I used suddenly to fall. I now promised St. Philomena to wear her cord, and begged her to cure me if such was God's will. She again came to my help, and I am once more well and happy, thank God.

A poor non-Catholic woman had her little girl at death's door. I spoke to her of St. Philomena and of the power of a Mass offered in her honor. Though very poor, she gave me a small stipend for the Mass, which a holy priest celebrated at my request. At once the danger passed, and the child is quite recovered. The poor mother tells everyone of the marvelous cure.

In thanksgiving I got a large statue of the Saint and offered it to our church.

These are a few of the many favors which I owe to this great Saint.

—M. G.

Presentation Convent, M.

Dear Rev. Father:

Please pardon what might seem to be an intrusion, but when I tell you that I am a devout client of St. Philomena, I feel that you will look on me as an old friend. Devotion to the little Wonder-Worker has been in a flourishing condition in this district for some years, but has got a distinct impetus during the past 12 months, owing to some very important cures, some of which seem truly miraculous.

Fortunately, we heard of the center established in the North Presentation Convent, Cork, from which we have been getting books, cords and leaflets. We were delighted with the little work, *St. Philomena—The Wonder-Worker*. It is indeed beautiful. I had read and re-read all I found on St. Philomena, but this little book took a real hold of me. It exercises a powerful influence on all who read it, and in truth no one could read it without being drawn to the dear Little Saint. It gave me much information which I had been eagerly longing for. Could you obtain for one of the priests here the faculty for blessing the cords of the Saint, which are eagerly sought after?

From a Roman Seminary

Dear Father:

You were kind enough to give us, when in Rome last year, the story of St. Philomena. It was read in the refectory, and the students very soon became intensely devout to the Wonder-Worker.

Our National Pilgrimage, as you remember, consisting of more than 2,000 persons, arrived in Rome in various groups shortly before the examinations, spending 10 days in the Eternal City. The students were allowed to assist the pilgrims as far as they could and take part in the various visits and devotions of the pilgrimage.

As a consequence, they lost much valuable time, and what was still worse, they naturally became very distracted.

Things looked gloomy indeed on the eve of the examinations. The first students who presented themselves cut a rather sorry figure, which increased the fear of the others.

As the result of a happy inspiration of one of our number, the remaining students made a solemn promise to St. Philomena to erect a statue of her in the College if all passed the examinations with *distinction!*

Certainly the request was a bold one! Thanks be to God, all not only passed, but some distinguished themselves, getting notably high marks.

I can safely say we never had, in all the years I have been in the College, such splendid results. St. Philomena, needless to add, has got her statue.

A second remarkable incident took place this year:

A well-intentioned friend, hearing the students speak in glowing terms of their great success, which all attributed to St. Philomena, and fearing that exaggeration in their devotion would result in prejudice to their studies, ventured to suggest that the proper way to guarantee good examinations was to study hard. Some six of the students misconstrued his remarks and in consequence grew lax in their devotions to our Saint; whereas, the others, though not neglecting their studies, continued to implore with fervor the assistance of the Wonder-Worker. The results were very significant. Those who placed their trust in the Wonder-Worker made splendid examinations; whereas, the others either barely got through or utterly failed. One of these latter had high hopes, shared in by professors and students alike, of achieving marked distinctions. He unfortunately failed so utterly as to be obliged to make another examination months later and possibly have to spend another year in Rome.

The Little Saint clearly showed how lovingly she protects her faithful friends.

—M. P.

The Following Letter Was Received from Dr. St. Helier Horgan.

Lisbon, August 3, 1926

My dear Father:

I have read the book you so kindly sent me: *St. Philomena—The Wonder-Worker.* I confess that it impressed me profoundly. I now pray to the Saint every day, and she gives me everything I ask. In gratitude for the extraordinary favors she has obtained for me, I have sent a large statue to my old college, where it was received with the greatest joy.

I am sending you the account of two very extraordinary favors which she granted to friends of mine, one to a Protestant naval officer, which I trust may be the cause of his conversion. When thanking me, he mentioned some difficulties which he had concerning the invocation of Saints. In answer, I sent him *St. Philomena—The Wonder-Worker*, which meets these difficulties perfectly.

In January, 1926, I learned that the name of this old shipmate of mine in the Navy had failed to appear on the promotion list for captain. He had only one more chance, on June 30, after which he would be obliged to leave the service if he did not get the desired promotion. That would spell dire calamity for a man with a family, for at his age and with his training, to what trade, to what profession could he turn for support? He was one of my greatest friends, a man of sterling qualities and great ability, but unfortunately with no luck and no influence. Everything seemed against him. There were 145 men for promotion, some with powerful political influence, others with a list of brilliant services in their favor. Of these, only ten would be promoted. I wrote to my friend, who was a Protestant. I felt what a state of suspense, almost despair, he must be in. I encouraged him, assuring him that I would pray daily to St. Philomena for his success and that I felt *absolutely certain* that she would hear my poor prayers, for I can truly say she has not yet refused me any favor. In a short time, I had a grateful letter announcing that, not only was my friend promoted, but he was actually second on the list! How did it happen? St. Philomena could tell if she only liked. I wish to publish my thanks to the Wonder-Worker for this new and striking favor, which I take as granted to me.

The last news is that my friend has entered the Catholic Church and that he has received a splendid promotion in the Navy.

The Following Is a Letter which I Received from a Friend in Cork. It Speaks for Itself.

July, 1926

My dear Doctor:

You have been in my mind a great deal lately, and why I have not written to you long ere this to announce the glad tidings of my wife's entire restoration to health I cannot understand.

Your friend and patron, St. Philomena, has been beyond doubt the Wonder-Worker. My dear wife is now free from her head noises (pronounced incurable), sleepless nervous depression and other ailments. Her digestive organs are working perfectly. The transformation commenced on the 25th of February.

Her troubles had been going on for 5 years, during which she was successively in the hands of seven clever doctors who, however, could do nothing for her. St. Philomena's life came to us from you. She read it at first in a very cursory manner while in bed, where she used to spend the greater part of her time. After reading it superficially, she put it on her table and appeared to forget all about it. She took it up again on the morning of the 25th of February, and this time read it with great avidity, so much so, that she could scarcely put it down. Finally, she went on her knees and prayed to the Saint to aid her in her great trouble. Every day after that, she read a part of the book and always seemed to find something new in it.

The doctor's visits had ceased for some time. At the end of a fortnight from the date of her prayer, she went to her doctor's house, who at first failed to recognize her, so improved had she become.

The old woman had disappeared, and a new woman was there. During all the five years of severe illness, she took no interest in her house or garden. Her maids did as they wished. Now you would not recognize the house. She insisted on improvements. The garden, which had been so neglected, is a picture. Visitors had been banned; now they are welcome. Our friends stop her in the streets in amazement at the change. The cure is not only complete, it is solid. In one sense, it is well that I have so delayed in communicating these facts to you, as I can now guarantee the stability of the change.

Believe me, dear Doctor, Yours very sincerely,
J. T.

Naples, August 26, 1926

Dear Rev. Father:

You will be pleased to read the following, which was published in this day's newspapers.

On the 2nd of October, 1925, the sculptor Luigi da Luca, while giving the finishing touches to a terra cotta statue of St. Philomena in the Church della Cesarea, was amazed to see the statue changing color.

He at once notified the rector of the church, and as a result the manifestations were made known to the ecclesiastical authorities for due investigation.

The Ecclesiastical Tribunal, after a thorough examination of the statue and a mature consideration of the facts, declared that the changes of color must be considered supernatural and miraculous.

The decision of the Ecclesiastical Tribunal was confirmed yesterday by the Cardinal Archbishop. Crowds are flocking to the Church, where the statue is exposed for view in the central chapel.

Yours truly,
C. P.

Appendix[2]

PRAYERS

NOVENA PRAYER TO SAINT PHILOMENA

O faithful virgin and glorious martyr, Saint Philomena, who works so many miracles on behalf of the poor and sorrowing, have pity on me. Thou knowest the multitude and diversity of my needs. Behold me at thy feet, full of misery, but full of hope. I entreat thy charity, O great saint! Graciously hear me and obtain from God a favorable answer to the request which I now humbly lay before thee. (*Here specify your petition.*) I am firmly convinced that through thy merits, through the scorn, the sufferings, the death thou didst endure, united to the merits of the Passion and Death of Jesus, thy Spouse, I shall obtain what I ask of thee, and in the joy of my heart I will bless God, who is admirable in His saints. Amen.

Nihil Obstat: Stephen Schapplcr, O.S.B.
Coadjutor Abbot, Imm. Conc. Prov.
Imprimatur: ✠ Charles Hubert Le Blond
Bishop of Saint Louis, January, 1952

2 Added by the Publisher to the 1993 edition.

THREE-PART NOVENA PRAYER

We beseech Thee, O Lord, to grant us the pardon of our sins by the intercession of Saint Philomena, virgin and martyr, who was always pleasing in Thy sight by her eminent chastity and by the profession of every virtue. Amen.

Illustrious virgin and martyr, Saint Philomena, behold me prostrate before the throne whereupon it has pleased the Most Holy Trinity to place thee. Full of confidence in thy protection, I entreat thee to intercede for me with God. Ah, from the heights of Heaven deign to cast a glance upon thy humble client! Spouse of Christ, sustain me in suffering, fortify me in temptation, protect me in the dangers surrounding me, obtain for me the graces necessary to me, and in particular (*here specify your petition*). Above all, assist me at the hour of my death. Saint Philomena, powerful with God, pray for us. Amen.

O God, Most Holy Trinity, we thank Thee for the graces Thou didst bestow upon the Blessed Virgin Mary, and upon Thy handmaid Philomena, through whose intercession we implore Thy Mercy. Amen.

Nihil Obstat: Rev. Leo J. Ward,
                  Censor Librorum
Imprimatur: ✠ Edward Cardinal Mooney
                  Archbishop of Detroit,
                  December 1, 1947

THE "LITTLE CROWN" OR CHAPLET
OF SAINT PHILOMENA

This chaplet consists of a **medal** of the Saint, **three white beads**—signifying virginity and in honor of the Blessed Trinity, for whose sake she laid down her life, and **thirteen red beads**—signifying martyrdom and commemorating the number of years Philomena lived on earth.

The "Little Crown" of Saint Philomena is a popular way of asking her help. This is prayed by saying first the **Apostles' Creed** to ask for the grace of faith. Then three **Our Fathers** are said, in honor of each of the three Divine Persons of the Blessed Trinity, in thanksgiving for the graces bestowed on Saint Philomena and for all the favors that have been obtained through her intercession. The following prayer is then repeated thirteen times to commemorate the thirteen years that Saint Philomena is supposed to have spent on earth:

Hail, O holy Saint Philomena, whom I acknowledge, after Mary, as my advocate with the Divine Spouse; intercede for me now and at the hour of my death.

Saint Philomena, beloved daughter of Jesus and Mary, pray for us who have recourse to thee.

The following prayer is said at the end of the Chaplet:

Hail, O illustrious Saint Philomena, who didst so courageously shed thy blood for Christ. I bless the Lord for all the graces He bestowed upon thee during thy life, and especially at thy death. I praise and glorify Him for the honor and power with which He has crowned thee, and I beg thee to obtain for me from God the graces I ask through thy intercession. Amen.

In praying the "Little Crown," it is suggested that one ask for the grace of purity in honor of the virginity of the Saint, who suffered death rather than tarnish this virtue; and secondly, for courage and fortitude to be faithful to the duties of a Christian, as she was.

PRAYER TO SAINT PHILOMENA FOR GROWTH IN VIRTUES

O glorious virgin, whose glory God has been pleased to make known by singular miracles, we address ourselves to thee with entire confidence! Obtain for us that, following thy example, we may fight courageously against whatever is opposed to the reign of Jesus Christ in our hearts; that we may adorn our souls with virtues like thine, particularly with that angelic purity of which thou art the perfect model; and that, inflamed with the love of Jesus, we may continually walk in the way which He has marked out, so that we may one day partake of thine everlasting happiness. Through our Lord Jesus Christ, who with the Father and the Holy Ghost lives and reigns, one God, in perfect Trinity, forever and ever. Amen.

Imprimatur for the "Little Crown" and the rest of this Appendix:

Nihil Obstat: Stephen Schappler. O.S.B.
                  Coadjutor Abbot, Imm. Conc. Prov.

Imprimatur: ✠ Charles Hubert Le Blond
                  Bishop of St. Joseph

PRAYER FOR PURITY

O glorious Saint Philomena, who, animated by a burning love for Jesus our Saviour, didst shine in Holy Church by the splendor of perfect virginity and the practice of the most heroic virtues, obtain for us of thy Divine Spouse the grace to keep ever unstained the precious treasure of chastity and to practice with generosity the virtues of our state, that having walked in His footsteps after thine example during our life on earth, we may rejoice in His glory with thee through all eternity.

Saint Philomena, happy virgin, adorned with all the charm of innocence, and beautified, besides, with the purple of martyrdom, obtain for us the grace to know how to suffer all and to sacrifice all in order to be faithful to God till death and possess Him eternally in Paradise. Amen.

PRAYER FOR THOSE WHO WEAR THE CORD OF SAINT PHILOMENA

O most pure virgin, glorious martyr, Saint Philomena, whom God in His eternal power seems to have revealed to the world in these disastrous days of ours in order to revive the faith, sustain the hope, and inflame the charity of Christian hearts, I kneel at thy feet. Deign, O kindest virgin, to receive my humble prayers, and to obtain for me that strength of soul which made thee resist the most terrible attacks of tribulation and suffering: that ardent love for Jesus which the most fearful sufferings could not extinguish in thy heart. Protect me in all the events of my life, from all dangers, spiritual and temporal. Be present with me also in my last hour, which I commend to thy loving charity with confidence, since in life I love thee and wear thy holy cord as a mark of my special devotion toward thee, the beloved of Jesus and Mary.

SHORT DAILY PRAYER FOR THOSE WHO WEAR THE CORD OF SAINT PHILOMENA

O Saint Philomena, virgin and martyr, pray for us, that through thy powerful intercession we may obtain that purity of mind and heart which leads to the perfect love of God. Amen.

LITANY OF SAINT PHILOMENA
Composed by St. John Vianney, the Curé of Ars.
(For private use only.)

Lord, have mercy on us.
Christ, have mercy on us.
Lord, have mercy on us. Christ hear us.
Christ, graciously hear us.
God the Father of Heaven,
Have mercy on us.
God the Son, Redeemer of the world,
Have mercy on us.
God the Holy Ghost,
Have mercy on us.
Holy Trinity, One God,
Have mercy on us.

Holy Mary, Queen of Virgins,
Pray for us.
Saint Philomena,
Pray for us.
Saint Philomena, filled with abundant graces from the cradle, *etc.*
Saint Philomena, model of virgins,
Saint Philomena, temple of the most perfect humility,
Saint Philomena, victim of the love of Christ,
Saint Philomena, example of strength and perseverance,
Saint Philomena, invincible athlete of chastity,
Saint Philomena, mirror of most heroic virtues,
Saint Philomena, firm and intrepid before torments,
Saint Philomena, scourged like thy Divine Spouse,
Saint Philomena, pierced by a shower of arrows,
Saint Philomena, consoled in chains by the Mother of God,
Saint Philomena, miraculously cured in prison,
Saint Philomena, sustained by angels in the midst of tortures,
Saint Philomena, who preferred humiliation and death to the splendor of a throne,
Saint Philomena, who converted the witnesses of thy martyrdom,
Saint Philomena, who wore out the fury of thine executioners,
Saint Philomena, patroness of the innocent,
Saint Philomena, patroness of youth,
Saint Philomena, refuge of the unfortunate,
Saint Philomena, health of the sick and infirm,
Saint Philomena, new light of the Church Militant,

Saint Philomena, who confounds the impiety of our age,

Saint Philomena, who reanimates the faith and courage of the faithful,

Saint Philomena, whose name is glorious in Heaven and terrible in Hell,

Saint Philomena, illustrious by the most splendid miracles,

Saint Philomena, powerful with God,

Saint Philomena, who reigns in glory,

Lamb of God, Who takest away the sins of the world, *Spare us O Lord.*

Lamb of God, Who takest away the sins of the world, *Graciously hear us, O Lord.*

Lamb of God, Who takest away the sins of the world, *Have mercy on us.*

V. Pray for us, Saint Philomena,

R. *That we may be made worthy of the promises of Christ.*

LET US PRAY

We beseech Thee, O Lord, to grant us the pardon of our sins by the intercession of Saint Philomena, virgin and martyr, who was always pleasing in Thy sight by her eminent chastity and by the profession of every virtue. Amen.

St. Philomena devotional articles (statues, chaplets, etc.) may be obtained from:

Mother of Our Savior Company
P. O. Box 100
Pekin, IN 47165

The Living Rosary Association
P. O. Box 1303
Dickinson, TX 77539

BOOKS BY
FATHER PAUL O'SULLIVAN, O.P.

HOW TO BE HAPPY—HOW TO BE HOLY

ALL ABOUT THE ANGELS

AN EASY WAY TO BECOME A SAINT

THE HOLY GHOST—OUR
GREATEST FRIEND

READ ME OR RUE IT

HOW TO AVOID PURGATORY

THE SECRET OF CONFESSION
Including The Wonders of Confession

THE WONDERS OF THE MASS

THE WONDERS OF THE HOLY NAME